2015
To Judy,
Merry Christmas!
Love always,
Matt

MY DEAR FRIEND

THE CIVIL WAR LETTERS OF

ALVA BENJAMIN SPENCER,

3RD GEORGIA REGIMIENT, COMPANY C

Edited by

Clyde G. Wiggins III

Mercer University Press
Macon, Georgia

© 2007 Mercer University Press
1400 Coleman Avenue
Macon, Georgia 31207
All rights reserved

First Edition.

Books published by Mercer University Press are printed on acid free paper
that meets the requirements of American National Standard for Information
Sciences—Permanence of Paper for Printed Library Materials.

Library of Congress Cataloging-in-Publication Data

Spencer, Alva Benjamin, 1840-1881.
My dear friend : the Civil War letters of Alva Benjamin Spencer, 3rd
Georgia Regiment, Company C / edited by Clyde G. Wiggins III. -- 1st ed.
p. cm.
Selections from the correspondence between Alva Benjamin Spencer and
Margaret Lucinda Cone.
Includes bibliographical references and index.
ISBN-13: 978-0-88146-057-5 (hardcover : alk. paper)
ISBN-10: 0-88146-057-5 (hardcover : alk. paper)
1. Spencer, Alva Benjamin, 1840-1881—Correspondence. 2. Soldiers—
Georgia—Correspondence. 3. Confederate States of America. Army. Georgia
Infantry Regiment, 3rd. Company C. 4. Confederate States of America. Army.
Georgia Infantry Regiment, 3rd. 5. Cone, Margaret Lucinda—Correspondence.
6. Georgia—History—Civil War, 1861–1865—Personal narratives.7. United
States—History—Civil War, 1861–1865—Personal narratives, Confederate.
8. Love-letters—Confederate States of America. 9. Couples—Georgia—Dooly
County—Correspondence. 10. Dooly County (Ga.)—Biography.
I. Wiggins, Clyde G. II. Cone, Margaret
Lucinda. III. Title.
E559.53rd .S64 2007
973.7'458—dc22
2007001907

To my wife Debbie, who I love more every day.

To my children, Holly and Brittany, who I hope will one day enjoy their family history as I do.

And to my parents, Clyde and Shirley, who are the best example of parents I know.

CONTENTS

PREFACE

Alva Benjamin Spencer

6 September 1840 – 20 May 1881

Mustered into service on 24 April 1861, Company C of the 3rd Georgia Regiment was made up of men of all ages from Greene County, Georgia. Under the command of Captain Robert L. McWhorter Sr., teenage boys to 60 year old men felt the call to serve their country in it's time of need. This company was to be known as the Dawson Grays.

Other units forming the 3rd Georgia included the Young Guards, Athens Guards, Home Guards, Governors Guards, Wilkerson Rifles, Brown Rifles, Confederate Light Guards, Caswell Guards, Dade Rifles, and the Burke Guards.

The men of Company C came from all walks of life. Fathers and sons, brothers, teachers, farmers, politicians, doctors and lawyers. Some well-to-do, others dirt poor. The only discriminating factors were age and color, and even those would be subject to speculation before the end of the war. Women and young girls did their part in helping with the war effort by managing the family farm, preparing shipments of food, knitting socks for the soldiers and in many other non-combat related ways.

Many of these men would never come home again, or if they did were often maimed physically or mentally. In later wars a solider might lose a friend he had known for a few months, but in this one you might lose a childhood friend, a brother, a father, or a son. These men fought in places and an environment many were entirely unfamiliar with. The early part of the war found them at Portsmouth, Virginia, and then on Roanoke Island, North Carolina. These boys who grew up running and playing on rock hard red Georgia clay, were now running and fighting in loose beach sand. Many who had never traveled far from their birthplace, let alone seen the ocean, found themselves now in a strange land. "Camp Rescue" they called it. One battle to be known as the "Chicimocomico Races" found them marching and running through beach sand described as being a "foot deep," for 20 miles one day, then back down the beach the next.

Alva's company would find themselves in many different places. Along with minor skirmishes, and in addition to Roanoke Island, they would fight in places such as South Mills (North Carolina), Seven Pines, Malvern Hill, Second Manassas, Sharpsburg, Fredricksburg, Chancellorsville, Gettysburg, Wilderness, the Battle of the Crater, Hatcher's Run, Spotsylvania, and Cold Harbor. The end of the war would take them to Appomattox, Virginia, for Lee's surrender.

Alva Benjamin Spencer was born in Penfield, Greene County, Georgia, 6 September 1840. He was the son of Benjamin Edgar Spencer, a shoemaker from Connecticut, and Charlotte Griffin Hurd, a native of Clinton, Middlesex County, Connecticut. What brought the Spencer's to Georgia is unknown, but it is possible Mr. Spencer may have come down for the Georgia Gold Rush or the Land Lottery with some of his brothers. Alva graduated from Mercer College, which at that time was in Penfield, Georgia, and was offered a job teaching school in the Dooly County, Georgia town of Millwood.

Alva traveled to Dooly County in a "two wheeled buggy," and moved onto the farm of Judge William Beacham Cone Sr. Judge Cone was a well known and highly respected leader in the community and had previously served in the 1847 Georgia Legislature.

It was on this farm that Alva would meet his future wife, Margaret Lucinda Cone, the daughter of W. B. Cone Sr. and Elizabeth Mobley. Alva and Margaret both taught school and became fast friends. Alva was often a guest for meals at the Cone family residence where Margaret and her sister Samantha would pass the time entertaining with their piano.

Life continued in this fashion for awhile until the Spring of 1861 when a 20 year old Alva answered the call of Georgia's Governor Joseph E. Brown and returned to Penfield. Anxious to fight he was not to be disappointed, as he would see the elephant many times over.

ACKNOWLEDGMENTS

Mr. Floyd Mashburn Turk
Waycross, GA

Mr. Turk (Alva's Great Grandson) owns the original letters and I am eternally grateful to him for his generosity in sharing these treasures with my family and giving us a chance to "communicate" with our ancestors. Additionally, Mr. Turk provided the original picture of Alva used in this book.

Mrs. Shirley Virginia (Spencer) Wiggins
Tallahassee, FL

Mrs. Wiggins (my Mother and Alva's Great Granddaughter) transcribed most of the letters in what she calls a "labor of love". Her painstaking attention to detail in the transcription has made this book possible. Mrs. Wiggins copied these letters word for word, and made no grammatical corrections to preserve their historical value. She has described many sessions of transcription that involved combinations of a magnifying glass and shining a light through the 140-year-old documents just to make out a single word.

Mr. John Ray Spencer
Kingman, AZ
25 April 1921 - 11 September 2006

Mr. Spencer (Uncle Ray to me and Alva's Grandson) transcribed some of these letters and provided some of the pictures in this book. Without Mr. Spencer's devotion to Spencer family research, much of what we know today would still be waiting to be discovered. The only thing I regret with the publication of this book, is that Uncle Ray is not here to hold it in his hands. I know he is watching from above and is as excited as I am.

Mrs. Mary Ruth Moore
Watkinsville, GA

Mrs. Moore provided the pictures of "Fannie," Alva's sister, and of Benjamin and Charlotte, Alva's parents.

ALVA BENJAMIN SPENCER
Used with the permission of John Ray Spencer.
Kingman, Arizona.

BENJAMIN EDGAR SPENCER AND CHARLOTTE GRIFFIN HURD.
Alva Benjamin Spencer's parents.
Used with the permission of Mary Ruth Moore.
Watkinsville, Georgia.

JULIA FRANCES (FANNIE) SPENCER.
Sister of Alva Benjamin Spencer.
Used with the permission of Mary Ruth Moore.
Watkinsville, Georgia.

that, on the march — I suppose they
will all leave before active operations
commence —

        Nothing of interest has trans-
pired since I last wrote, save the reenlistment of our Brigade for the war,
the 3rd Ga. taking the lead, the rest
following — Almost the entire corps
of Gen. A. P. Hill have reenlisted —
Those who didn't reenlist, have, by a recent
act of Congress, been conscripted —

        My respects to Miss Sis — The
mail is about to leave so I must
close — Love to all — Hoping to see
or hear from you soon I remain
as ever Yours devotedly

                A. B.

Camp "Jennie Hart" Virginia
23rd February 1864

Dear Maggie

      I've delayed writing to you for sometime, hoping that very soon, I should have the exquisite pleasure of answering your last in "propria persona"; but it now seems that I'm doomed to disappointment, again — Our furloughs have been gone, now, six or seven days, and it does seem as if they were gone for good — They will certainly be in this evening, or not at all —

      A day or two since I received a letter from Father informing me that Mother had received a severe fall, and he was afraid that it might prove serious — I haven't received any additional information since his first announcement — This information makes me more than ever anxious to receive our furloughs —

MARGARET LUCINDA CONE SPENCER *(top)*, WILLIE JANETTE BROWN SPENCER
(left-Margaret's daughter in law), WILLIE ELMER SPENCER *(right- Margaret's grandson)*,
and MARGARET LOUISE SPENCER *(bottom- Margaret's granddaughter,*
who died shortly after this picture was made).
Circa early 1907. Used with the permission of John Ray Spencer. Kingman, Arizona.

SAMANTHA JANE CONE MOBLEY.
Sister of Margaret Lucinda Cone.
Used with the permission of Floyd Mashburn Turk.
Waycross, Georgia.

CHAPTER 1

1861

In this early part of the war Alva has seen first-hand what can become of your sincere thoughts put on paper when the enemy captures your mail. It is believed that perhaps the reason we have so few letters in this early part of the war is that he asked Margaret to destroy his and vowed to do the same to hers. He felt it a crime to destroy hers, but felt he must to prevent them falling into the wrong hands. Later letters were mailed to his sister for safe keeping.

In reading the regimental history of the 3rd Georgia, as written by Charles Andrews the Regimental Historian, it is this writers opinion that when Spencer and Andrews write of the same event, Spencer's account could be taken as more accurate. Alva most often wrote of things as they were occurring, most of the time the same day, or within days. From what I can determine, Andrews account was written at a later date. In one instance in this first chapter, Alva writes of something that occurred on his birthday, something that you would tend to remember. Andrews, in his account of the same events, list this as occurring a week later. As the war gets underway, Alva relays information of a soldiers life, recounts a story he's heard of the death of Gen. Ellsworth, a good friend of President Lincoln, and oh how they detest Roanoke Island. Anything to get off that island and back to Portsmouth where he say's he could almost "live" off oysters. One wonders if he would turn up his nose at a waterfront house there today?

Alva kept a diary, however only a short part from September to October of 1861 has been found. Entries can be found at the beginning of the closest letter to the entry date. Enlisting in Company C of the 3rd Georgia Regt. on April 29, 1861, Alva had to purchase his own uniform in Atlanta. His father, Benjamin Edgar Spencer, is in the same unit and is already in Portsmouth, VA. Alva returns home to Penfield, GA before leaving for war, and writes the first letter we have to a fellow school teacher in Millwood (Dooly County), GA., Margaret Lucinda Cone.

A gentleman's war if nothing else, Alva announces that "all cursing & swearing are prohibited."

Penfield, Georgia
13th May 61
My dear Friend
According to promise I now proceed to write you a few lines. After arriving in Montezuma[1] I had the pleasure of meeting with some of my old acquaintances. The "Military Company" the "Hardee Rifles" were on the train when it passed the depot. When I arrived in Atlanta I purchased my outfit for the war. I had also the pleasure of seeing Gen. Beauregard[2] and hearing him speak. He is a very small man; about as large as Mr. Henry. He is no orator; but a perfect model of a warrior.

After coming home I made all the necessary arrangements for leaving. My Mother hates for me to go, but does not object. My sister will accompany me to Augusta. We leave this morning.

There was a fire in town the night after I came. There were three houses burnt (out-houses); and the dwellings were in great danger; but by the untiring efforts of the students and citizens, the fire was extinguished before any serious damage was done.

We received a letter from Pa and other members of our Company on Saturday. One of the company has the measles. The rest in fine health. They are stationed in Portsmouth opposite

---

[1] Montezuma GA.
[2] General Pierre Gustave Toutant (P.G.T.) Beauregard, CSA

Norfolk. The order to Richmond was countermanded by Gov. Letcher of Va. When I shall have arrived there I will write all the news. Please answer immediately and not put it off as you do Mat. Poole. Give the rest of the family and other inquiring friends - Direct (?) to your friend.

A.B.Spencer
Portsmouth
Virginia
Care
Capt. McWhorter
3rd Regiment
"Dawson Greys"

Portsmouth, Va.
May 20th 1861
Miss Margaret
Dear Madam;

According to promise I proceed to give you some account of my travel to this place. Situated as I am, you will no doubt excuse all improprieties and mistakes that I may make.

I have been at this place for three days; but it seems to me to be almost an age. I tell you we have a very hard time indeed. It is true we have the greatest of plenty to eat; but we have to work on our batteries in the day, and stand guard at night rain or shine. It is true I have a hard time but I am very well satisfied with my lot. We are situated just behind the "Gasport Navy Yard". You doubtless recollect the circumstances under which the abolitionists left it. They attempted to burn it; and in fact did burn a part, but the remainder is said to be worth about forty millions of dollars. Those troops stationed in the "yard" have raised one large war vessel, and are preparing it as a floating battery, to float in Elizabeth river at this place. There are stationed in and around this place also around Norfolk about ten or twelve thousand troops mostly Georgians. I went to Norfolk the other day and could plainly see "Craney Island" and "Fort Norfolk", at which places are stationed a great many troops. There was a little brush between the Confederate and Federal troops yesterday, about 12 or 18 miles below this place. It is supposed that the Federal ship was struck. Nobody on our side hurt. We could distinctly hear the cannonading from this point. Some suppose there will be an engagement in less than ten days; but I can hardly believe it; although things look like pretty *"tight papers"*[3]. I think we have a very good situation, and are, or will be, very well fortified in a few days. There are in the "Navy Yard" a great many cannon - several thousand, some of the largest kind. There is enough timber in the yard to build thirty war vessels. The workmen in the Navy Yard are moulding cannon, and musket balls all the while. I have heard some say, we had no arms; it is not so. We have more arms than we know what to do with. In our encampment there are about one thousand troops. Furney Poole, and Jno. Roundtree are among the number. I see a great many of my old acquaintances in camp.

We have *bacon, crackers, sugar, coffee, salt, beef, meal, fish, syrup, pies cake, peas, etc.* We can buy as many fish as we can carry, for a cent apiece.

I will endeavor to write as often as possible. *You* know I have very little time to do such. Give my best respects (to) the family, and everybody else. Write soon to me as below.

Yours most *respectfully*,
A.B.Spencer
Portsmouth, Va.
3 Reg. Geo. Vol.
Capt. McWhorter
Dawson Greys

---

[3] Meaning a "sure thing", or most likely to happen.

Portsmouth, Va.
Camp Gwinn
May 28th, 1861
Dear Friend

I received your most kind and welcome lines yesterday evening & have read & reread its contents, each time finding something to admire. I am truly glad to hear that your company is progressing so finely. I hope ere long to meet it on the field of battle. That is a friendly meeting. I should like to know how my school is getting on; whether or no there is any one teaching in my place; if not, I hope so; for I hate for the people to be disappointed by anything I do. I thought it to be my duty or I never would have done as I did.

We are getting along finely since I've been in camp. I have been a little sick; but not seriously so. There have been several cases of measles in our camp since I've been out. All over now convalescing.

Camp life is a hard one sure; but I never complain. We live hard & work hard. We drill some six hours every day. Sometimes we stand guard all day & all night. If anyone is found asleep on his post, the penalty is death. If he gets intoxicated he is compelled to stand guard two days & nights. All cursing & swearing are prohibited. There have been several engagements between the Federal & Confederate Troops below us ten or twelve miles. The Confederate troops at "Sewell's Point" fired into the ship Monticello, disabling her very much and killing six men and wounding several others. Nobody hurt on our side.

The other day the Confederate troops stationed at York River, or near there, seeing the Federal steamer "Yankee" concealed in a small vessel several hundred troops and succeeded in capturing her. They towed her to Petersburg.

Not long since, an Army of Federal troops marched to Alexandria, Va., to a Hotel[4] where a Confederate flag was flying. Col.

---

[4] The Marshall House.

Ellsworth,[5] the Commander of the Federal troops, seized the flag, marched to Jackson[6], the Hotel keeper, remarking that he had a prize; whereupon Jackson, the hotel keeper, remarked he had a prize too and fired upon Ellsworth killing him immediately. The Federal troops being enraged killed Jackson forthwith. The wife of Jackson having seized the "Confederate Flag", was ordered to throw it down. She refused and was threatened with death if she did not comply. She then tore the flag to pieces and dared them to shoot; but I don't think they did.

Federal troops are supposed to be landing below here in considerable numbers. The enemies' troops are stationed at "Fortress Monroe" about 18 miles below this place. So you see we are not very far from each other. I wouldn't care if we were still nearer to each other. Our *Boys* are anxious for a fight. We keep everything ready to march to any place at a moment's warning. We were called from this place to a station on the railroad about 8 miles above here called "Bowers Hill". The enemy was thought to be marching on this place. I think we were ready in 15 minutes after the order was given. Upon arriving at our destination we marched some two or three miles, in a very hard rain; but found no "Lincolnites".

We get no news here, the officers don't let us know anything, and we are prevented from going outside of a certain boundary without a pass signed by two men.

There are 10 companies here composing the 3rd Reg. Among them are Furney Poole, Jno. Roundtree & Charlie Bass from Hayneville. A brother of Jack Pound's is here besides a great many others with whom I am acquainted. I have a gay time.

Give my love to every body & tell them to write as I have very little time. I have to write with a pencil. Excuse if you please.

Your true friend
A.B.Spencer
Portsmouth, Va.

---

[5] Colonel Elmer Ephraim Ellsworth, USA
[6] James Jackson.

Care
Capt. McWhorter
3rd Reg.Geo. Vol.
Dawson Greys

Camp Gwynn, Va.
June 25, 1861
My dear Friend

I rec'd. yours a few days since, and in compliance with your request I will now try and give you some account of our present situation and the prospects for a fight at this place. In the first place, let me say I *could* write more than I will in this letter; but for the reason that I don't know whether the reports current are true or false.

You no doubt get the correct accounts of battles fought in this state before I do; consequently what I write will be an "Old song" before reaching you.

We are stationed near two cities it is true; but we have so little communication with citizens, that we hear but little concerning military operations, and what we hear is not all reliable. Whenever there is any engagements below we can hear very distinctly the booming of the canon; but the balance is all conjecture, that is where and between whom, it is taking place.

Yesterday I went down the Elizabeth River, in a steamer, to "Craney Island"; from which place I could, with the assistance of a telescope, see very plainly the Federal fleet, and "Fortress Monroe". I counted from 25 to 30 vessels large and small with the "Stars and Stripes" floating from their masts. I could also (see) an innumerable number of tents scattered along the beach. Some of the vessels were very large indeed; at least they appeared so to me considering the great distance I was from them, ten miles. I saw two large war steamers blockading James River. They were lying directly across the channel. From Craney Island I could see "Sewell's Point",

"Newport.News", "Hampton", and "Pig's Point". The two points are occupied by Confederate troops; the others by Federal troops. That Lincoln has a great many troops stationed in Va., there is no doubt; but we are not at all frightened. All we ask is to give us a "fair showing" and we will whip the last one and drive them back to their "dens" in ---- "double quick time"- We (are) superior to them in strength of arms- if not in number.

As to there being an engagement at this place by water, is absolutely prepostorous as the city of Norfolk is almost entirely surrounded by strong batteries, and regiments of infantry and cavalry. The whole fleet of Abraham combined with that of England can not possibly pass up the river to "Gasport Navy Yard". I say they could not for this reason; they will be compelled to pass some six or eight batteries, one of them Craney Island mounting 35 or 40 of the largest guns, the others each ---- 15 to 20 guns, all bearing directly upon the channel. Besides these batteries, several large vessels have been sunken in the channel between Norfolk and the island. If Lincoln's troops should succeed in passing the island they will have to pass other strong batteries "viz" ""Ft. Norfolk" "Pindors Point" "Fort Nelson" and two strong batteries at the Navy Yard. One of the two at the yard is a ship turned into a battery.

The laborers in the yard have succeeded in raising the "Merrimac"[7] a large screw propeller war steamer and will have raised to-morrow the sloop of war "Plymouth". They are also at work raising the "Germantown" a very good vessel.

While raising the "Plymouth" one of the workmen was accidentally killed. He was working under the water in a "Submarine armor" and the head piece was accidentally unscrewed, and he was drowned before they could get him out. It was a sad accident indeed. He leaves a wife and four small children to mourn his loss. A brass band has been formed for the regiment and I am a member. We have 10 members. We are getting along with it finely. One thing I like it

---

[7] Merrimack. An abandoned Union ship, later cristened the "Virginia" by the Confederate Navy.

for is that we get better pay than the privates. We will probably leave this place and be quartered at some other point now soon. I have got to that point now that I don't care where I go or when. Leading a soldier's life is not altogether such as I anticipated; but I had much rather be here than at home, on account of the excitement there. I know they are in more suspense about our being engaged in a battle than we are.

I heard the other day that the Pulaski company had come to Virginia; but I haven't as yet heard to what point they have gone.

I rec'd a letter, since yours, from Mr. Henry. He gave me a pretty good description of affairs in Millwood[8]. He told me that my old school house was the store house for the "Light infantry". I don't suppose it is quite as dull around that place as formerly, but I expect it is equally as instructive as ever, in one department.

Tell Jack, Thom, Robts, and the rest of the boys that they must not come with the expectation of living as well here as at home it is all a mistake. It is true they will get a plenty to eat and good sleeping apartments; but the thing that is worst of all is the dull monotony. We have to go over the same thing each day, and it necessarily makes one sigh for the delicious comforts of home. They will however soon get used to it and get so lazy that they can not quit eating when they get started. If they, or any one else becomes a soldier they will get very lazy. It is not like the common laziness lasting for a day or two when it is hot weather but it lasts all the time and Sunday too. Tell Jack and the boys they need not be scared of bringing too much money, they will have use for all they can get, and more besides. I mean it is the case with us stationed here, and presume it is the same with the others. We sometimes want some little things besides bacon and bread and must buy it with our own money. I should like very much to see your company, and hope to do so soon on the battle field of our common country. Give my respects (to) Miss *Sis*, Miss Mat L., John, Joe, your father, brothers Sisters, mother, Robt. and all my friends in and around Millwood. Tell Mr. Henry I will answer his

---

[8] Millwood, GA (Dooly County).

letter as soon as possible. Tell your father to write to me as it would be quite welcome to me in my present situation, as I am always ready to receive, if not to answer, letters. The reason I am so dilatory in writing is that I have so little time. I will try and write again soon. Write again soon and give me all the news. All of you must write.

Yours most respectfully,
A.B.Spencer
Portsmouth, Va.
3rd Reg. Ga. Vol.
Company C.

Camp Gwynn, Va.
July 7th, 1861
Dear Friend:

I rec'd. your kind & interesting letter a good long time since and would have answered it previous to now, but for want of time. I have just said it was for want of time. I mean for want of energy. I tell you the truth that I can't compose my mind enough to write anything interesting.

The other day we all went off on a war tramp again. It was not exactly a war tramp but a 4th of July excursion to a point opposite "Old point comfort", old Abe's headquarters. It was perfectly surrounded by vessels of every description. They are bringing in forces to that place every day. It is impossible to tell the exact number of troops stationed at "Fortress Munroe" but it is certain that there is a great number, After we stopped we were met by 2 other Regiments besides 2 cavalry & 1 artillery company. They were reviewed by the officers and marched around several times, after which the artillery company fired several times. I stood the trip very well indeed. My feet were a little sore; but not as much as some of the other boy's. Some of them were completely blistered from toe to heel. I tell you I can stand it about as well as any one else in the Regt.; if I am of such small stature. I have been sick only two days since here I've been.

The Regt. has, previous to this time, been in very bad health; but it is now in a very good condition, some few are sick.

We have taken down our tents & have moved them about two hundred yards from their former position. I like the present place much better than the former. It is situated in ten feet of the river and consequently is very cool; at least much more so than the former place.

I suppose you have ere this heard of the fights that have taken place in western Va. and know more of them than I am able to tell you. I heard that Ex. Gov. Wise had taken prisoners one of Old Abe's Companies, and that they had given up their arms. After this the captain of the company told Wise he would fight for the South if he (Wise) would give him his arms again. Wise consented, and him & his comp. in his Regt. I say this is the report, I don't know whether it is correct or not. I give it only for what it is worth. It is reported that McGruder[9] was killed & his troops completely routed at Newport News. I say the same of this as the other. Last night at about twelve oclock several Signal rockets were seen to go up into the air. Some of them were red, some blue & some white; consequently there must have been an engagement down the river at some point below this place. I haven't heard from there; but it is nevertheless my opinion that such has been the call; I will probably hear some report this evening whether true or not. I can not tell. That which confirms me in my opinion is that we heard cannon down the river this morning very distinctly. These reports may be true, I hope they are, but you needn't put the utmost confidence in them from my say so. Give my respects to every body in the neighborhood of my acquaintance, and tell them I should like very much to hear from them at any time. If they only knew how much pleasure it afforded me they would certainly write to me often. It is true I have very little time to write, nevertheless I promise to write whenever I can possibly do it. Probably you will not believe me when I say that I've not written home in over a month, it is however true.

---

[9] Major General John B. Magruder, CSA

Yesterday the Regt. marched into town to hear a speech from Judge Jos. H. Lempkin of Ga. He gave us quite a nice speech ----. You must now excuse me. I hope to hear from you soon and all the news.

I remain your most obdt. servt.

A.B.Spencer
Portsmouth, Va.
Care
Capt. McWhorter
3rd Reg. Geo. Vol.

"Camp Gwynn" Portsmouth, Va.

13th July 1861

Dear Friend

Your kind and interesting letter of the 4th was rec'd. yesterday, and I now proceed to *try* and answer it in such a way as may interest you.

In the first place I will have to ask your pardon and beg that you will excuse me for not answering your other letter before now. I have no valid excuse to offer; indeed none of any sort; only laziness, of which I am ashamed; I am truly glad to know that neglecting to write does not cause you to "count letters", as you used to speak about. Excuse me this time and I will try and do better next time.

I am glad to hear that the D.L.I. have been ordered out. That is I am glad on their account; but sorry for their relatives. I can sympathize with you in parting with your relatives and friends, as I have passed through the same "ordeal". I suppose you now have some slight conception of my feelings when leaving my friends in Dooly, and especially those upon leaving my mother and sister. I know you felt emotions of regret upon my leaving; yet if I were certain that yours was as strong as mine I would then *know* that there were those whose respect for me could not be diminished by being separated from each other so a distance and for so long a time perhaps forever.

I don't want you to think now that I am dissatisfied with my lot, far from it. I am just as well satisfied with my present situation as I could possibly be at any other place in the world except ----, you may guess the balance.

In yours you said something about the place at which I spent the last 4th July hinting that I was at Miss Mollie's. I confess being there on that day, and would like to have been there on the last, if I had been in the same circumstances as then. But you know circumstances alter cases.

I will now write something I don't wish you to mention; but there is no use in asking you to keep it a secret as I know you will keep it, without you have grown out of your old way. I know you have been able to keep one and I now believe you can still keep one. I confess I was once in love with Mollie, and thought I had good reason to believe that it was reciprocated; but alas for "human weakness" I found that I was most awfully deceived. It may be a fortunate thing for me; yet I can't but help loving her as formerly, and still I know it's no use. If I can't call her my own, I *can say* she is one of the most loveable women of my acquaintance. There is something about the woman that captivates a person before he is aware of it, or even while he is just forming her acquaintance. She is indeed a fit subject for producing "love at first sight". You no doubt thought that we were more strongly attached to each other than we really were, and indeed we would have been if we could; but we couldn't if we would. Enough of this foolishness, I know you will not be interested in such things.

You no doubt think that I, stationed away off here in the very centre of the war, would have a great quantity and also a great variety of news to communicate to you; but it is all a mistaken idea. It is true I hear a great deal of news; but it is hard to separate the true from the false and consequently

I write none, as I don't wish to write you any *lies*. If anything I shall write proves to be false, attribute it to an error of my head and not of my heart. I have no doubt but that you get the correct reports in Millwood before we get them here. You see that we not being allowed to go to town are necessarily prevented from getting the correct reports of battles which have taken place in fifty or sixty miles, nay in 20 or 30 miles of our own camp. It looks a little surprising; yet it is nevertheless the truth "if it were not so I would have told you". If I had a mind to, I could write a whole volume of false reports; but I will desist. The other (day) we heard a report that there was an engagement below here in which three thousand Federal troops were slain. In a day or two it was totally contradicted. I give this only as a sample of the way in which we get all our news. It is true these reports sometimes prove to be true; but most generally they prove to be false.

Since your brothers and friends have left home and expect to come to Va., I've no doubt you will be interested in whatever transpires in war; at least much more so than you have been heretofore. If they are ordered to this state they will probably come to this place, as ours is the only Regt. here at the "Navy Yard". If they do not come here, but to some place near here, I will do all in my power to see them and give them some "dots" as I will be a little better versed in the science of war than they are and consequently will be able to give them some advice that may profit them a little if attended to. I hope they will come as nothing would please me more than to be with in such a glorious cause. You no doubt have heard, if not you will, something relative to the dissatisfaction expressed by some against our Colonel. I will try and give you as correct and as unbiased account of it as I can.

As soon as all the companies composing this Regt. were all here, an election for field officers was held, and the following names were elected, for Col. A. R. Wright, Lieutenant Col. Jas. L. Reid, Major A. H. Lee, and ADJT. W. W. Turner. This difficulty arose from Capt. Blodget not being elected. On account of this, he drew up a petition requesting him to resign. Some 300 signed it. You will see in the papers that 7 or 800 signed it. This is an infamous lie, excuse profanity. This petition was not handed to the Col.; but he hearing that such a project was on foot, made a speech to the Regt. in which he would not resign so long as he had power in his arm to wield his sword. He told us he would enter into an investigation of the affair and see who were engaged in it threatening to make them suffer for it. After hearing this speech Capt. Blodget of the "Blodget Volunteers" stepped forward and gave up his sword. Col. Wright upon receiving it told him to consider himself under arrest. It is believed by some that Capt. Blodget wrote an account of this affair himself and sent it to Augusta for publication. Whether this be true or not I can not tell but I believe it to be such. A "Court Martial" has been called and is now in session. I have not heard the result of its deliberations but it is generally believed that his commission will be taken from him and he be sent home in disgrace. I am very sorry indeed that such a thing has happened; but as it is the case I am for settling it immediately, in what way I care not. I only hope that justice will be meted out to all parties concerned.

The other day the Regt. under an order from Col. Wright struck their tents and moved from their old camp ground to a place up the river some hundred yards from our old camp. The present situation is a much pleasanter one than the former being in a position favorable to receiving the sea breezes. This too has been one cause of my not answering your letter. You see if I keep on finding excuses I will soon have enough to exculpate myself.

Now that we have become settled I will try and make my correspondence more interesting than the present or any previous to this time.

Our band is progressing finely. We now number eleven and expect several more. We play some pieces *quite* well. Of course, I am a good judge being myself a member. We don't have much playing to do for the Regt.; but we are all the time practicing, consequently we have no time to do anything else.

The health of this Regt. has been remarkably good compared with that of others. There have been only 3 or four deaths since we've been stationed here, while at others there have been a great many. Before we left home we supposed this to be a very unhealthy place; but so far it has proven to be quite as healthy as any place we could have gone, in fact it is more so. It is true we have had a great deal of sickness, measles, etc., but no dangerous diseases, have been made known as yet.

You were kind enough in your last to give me some account of the manner in which you spent the fourth of July. I will try and return the favor, if it will in any way interest you. Our Regt. on that day marched down the river to a point some ten or twelve miles distant, where we constructed some rude tents of brushes and prepared for rest. We slept on the cold ground covering ourselves with the blankets we brought strapped upon our persons. Rising at day-break next morning, we prepared our breakfast from the three days "rations" that we carried with us; and very soon after we marched to the encampment of the fourth Geo. Regt.; where we were met by two other Regts., two Cavalry companies and one Artillery. It was a larger collection of soldiers than I have ever seen before. After marching around several times, and firing the artillery pieces as fourth of July salutes, we returned to our temporary tents.

The next morning at one oclock we started back to this place. From our temporary encampment down on the river we could plainly see 4 points occupied by the Federal troops. Those points are "Fortress Monroe" the rendezvous of Lincoln's hirelings, "Newport News", "Rip Raps", and Hampton, the latter possessing one of the most beautiful college buildings I ever saw in my life. The Fortress was surrounded by vessels of the largest kinds. The college at Hampton was taken from Virginia by the Federal troops, and now it's walls echo to the revelinqs of a ruthless soldiery.

We could see also four points occupied by Confederate troops viz "Pigs point", "Sewells point", "Griners battery", and "Craney Island". If you could see the unanimity of feeling and anxiety of the soldiers in the Confederate Army, you could not for a moment doubt the certainty of a glorious victory soon. We have "thrashed them out" in every engagement so far and by the help of God will continue to do so until peace is declared. Are there many in your neighborhood that refused to join in the company? If there are I should think they would fare rather badly, if the ladies are as patriotic in Dooly as they are in old Greene[10], of which I doubt not. In our town the ladies have formed themselves into a society for the protection of those *young men* left behind, refusing to come. I would not be at home now to stay for any length of time for one thousand dollars.

We have had thirty recruits added to our company since we have been out. Our Regt. now numbers about one thousand and fifty. Our Regt. is considered about here to be one of the best drilled regts. from GA, VA, N.C., or La. I hope we will continue to enjoy such a reputation during the whole campaign.

I am sorry to know that Miss Louisa has been guilty of having the blues. I understood her to tell me that she would not *take on* much when the boys left. Tell her if she wants to get cured, she must write to me, and after receiving mine she would get mad, which is a much better disease than being blue. You said that Red took on considerable. I've doubt that you were the sole cause of his grief- don't get mad. We are faring most sumptuously now. We have *bacon*, fresh meat, and almost every kind of vegetables that we desire. The other day we had our provision box replenished by a box from home containing butter, cake, ham and the *best* of all some *wine*. After this we had a fine dinner, and the presence of some very nice gentleman. If what I have written interests you I have attained my object, so you must excuse me for the present. Give my love to Miss Mat when you see her, also to Miss Sis, the family, and everybody else of my acquaintance.

Your true friend

A.B.Spencer

---

[10] Greene County, GA

"Camp Gwynn" Va.

12th August 1861

My dear friend:

I am well at present, and hope these few lines will find you enjoying the same rich blessing. After this startling intelligence, I hope you will be able to receive whatever of a milder nature that may come after. Probably you are beginning to think that I have forgotten you entirely; but when I tell you that *you* are the only lady, outside of my immediate family, to whom I've written, you will think I have remembered you at least. I ---- as any of my *friends*- I haven't even written to "Mollie".

I have been waiting until now to try and give you some account of the recent battles fought in Virginia, although I doubt not that you have received more correct and more interesting accounts from Your friend at Manassas than I could possibly give you.

In the first place I will try and give you some account of our own situation, and then, if I can, I will give you some account of the condition of others.

We are stationed at the same old place, and are going through the same dull routine of duties from morning till night. The most objectionable feature in a camp life is the monotony. Each day we have the same duties to perform as the preceding. It is very rarely the case that we have anything novel to engage our minds, consequently we become lazy both in body and mind. No doubt you've discovered this in the substance and execution of my letters. If you haven't I hope it will continue to be the case; for it is my highest' ambition to please and interest those for whom I entertain such an exalted opinion as yourself. One company from our Regt. has been transferred to another stationed at Manassas. This company is the one that has caused so much disturbance in our Regiment, and I'm truly glad it has left us. It is called the "Blodget Volunteers". Another company has been sent to fill its place. I think it is a worse set than the other. Col. Wright has sent to President Davis to see if he cannot ---- off from accepting them. I hope he will succeed in doing so.

All the members of this Regt. seem to be very anxious to be ordered to some point where they can make known to the "Yankees" the fact that the "Rebels", as they unanimously call us, have some little left. I should like it myself if I could be nearer the seat of war than I am; but if the "powers that be" think it best that we should remain where we now are, I shall wait patiently my time. If I should be so lucky as to return home safe and sound, I will have the satisfaction of knowing that I was, during the war, protecting one the most valuable pieces of property in the Southern Confederacy, namely, "Gasport Navy Yard". The battles fought recently in this state are the most terrible of the nineteenth century. The number killed and wounded on both sides never will be actually known. We conjecture, suppose, and expect that the enemy's loss was terrible; but we have no means of correctly ascertaining the correct amount. Some of their news papers have acknowledged 20,000, others not so much, and others more. The number of canon, small arms, ambulances, and other accoutrements of war was incredible. In the wagons there was a great quantity of provisions. We also took about 30,000 handcuffs. The object of these handcuffs is not known. Some of their prisoners say they were for suppressing rebellion; but the most current opinion is that they were intended for our troops taken in the engagement. In some of the enemies knapsacks were found envelopes ornamented with very strange devices. Some were ornamented with the representation of a "Federal Soldier" bearing the "Stars & Stripes", and underneath were the words "Onward to Richmond". In another was found a rope halter, attached to which was a card containing the words "Tight rope performance at Richmond" "Admittance free". No doubt these fiendish hirelings expected soon to be in Richmond as conquerors; but thanks to God their designs were fraughted. If the Federals had been victorious at Manassas and other points not many of us would have lived to see the end of the war. But as it is, I think everything will be peace and quiet in twelve months, and we all will be permitted to return home in Glory. Some think there will be a great many battles fought yet but I beg leave to differ- I may however be wrong. I knew a great many that were killed and wounded in that battle. Some of my most intimate friends were there. The most glorious thought to Georgians is that the 7th & 8th Georgia Regts. acted so nobly. They covered themselves with glory. The name of the gallant Bartow will ever be a household word in the history of our own beloved Georgia. He died while gallantly leading on his troops to victory, and his last words were "boys they have killed me, but don't give up the battle". Nor must I pass over the names of those brave heroes; Beauregard and Johnston. It is said that Beauregard's horse being shot from under him and the battle seeming to be in the balance, he was so intensely excited as to render himself perfectly miserable. Soon, however, his misery was turned to happiness when he saw the enemy fleeing so precipitously before his exhausted soldiers "like lean sheep before hungry wolves", if you will allow the expression. In the flight one of Lincoln's congressmen was thrown from his horse, and being overtaken by one of our cavalrymen was compelled to get up behind him and join in the pursuit of his men. On returning the cavalryman amused himself by causing his horse to kick up to the extreme annoyance and fear of the Yankee. The Yankees so sure of success that they had even prepared a sumptuous feast for themselves; but contrary to their expectations, we received the feast instead of themselves. The battle ground, or the stream near it was formerly called "Bloody Run"; but it is now more appropriately styled the "Big Run", from the run of the Yankees. I have seen several that have been on the battle ground since the engagement and they say they never saw such a sight in their lives. The ground is literally covered with the dead bodies of men and horses. The graves of the Yankees can be easily distinguished from those of the Confederates, the former are merely thrown into the holes dug for them in any way. Sometimes an arm or a foot or a head is left uncovered & exposed to the sun's hot rays. Those of our men are marked by a board, at the head and feet, with the name of the inmate written or cut upon its surface. This one thing shows the difference of the two parties. The one being a civilized party the other a barbarous party. Oh, what a pity it is that we have to take lives of so many men in fighting against so many friends. One army being composed of the flower of the country, the other of the surfs and prisoners of the north. The greater number of the prisoners taken at the battle ground are at Richmond. Most of them say they would fight against us no more. Some, however, say they would fight us again if they were once more free. As to the movements of Beauregard no one knows anything about them, but I believed, pretty generally, that he intends making an attack upon Washington. How true it is I can not say. I know, however, that there is some grand movement on foot and we will soon know all about it.

You have no idea of the fun I see here in Virginia every day. I have several days taken rides in boats with ladies up and down the Elizabeth river. There are some very nice young ladies in this vicinity that is in and around Portsmouth and Norfolk. I am acquainted with several nice ones and enjoy myself finely. I don't like the ladies in this state altogether as well as those in Georgia. The people generally seem to be pretty sociable but there are a great many here not of the right stripe. I mean to say there are a good many abolitionists here. Leastwise, the blacksmiths in the navy yard struck of for a very slight excuse, in fact you may call it no excuse on account of this Genl. Huger has detailed all kinds of workmen. The different Regiments around this place to work in the navy yards. These men who quit the yard said if any of our boys went to work in the yard they would burned it up. Hearing this, Col. Wright sent out a police guard into town, and our whole regiment slept with our arms, prepared for an attack from these men at any moment in the night. There are about one thousand men at work in the yard, and it was supposed that a great many would sympathize with these blacksmiths and that they would endeavor to commit some incendiary act.

In your last you said something in reference to Nancy writing to me. I hope I will not have to ask her to write to me any more before I receive one. When I left she promised me that she would certainly write, and still she hasn't written yet; but I hope next time to receive a long, long one. I don't mean now for you and Nancy to get mad at this; for I think you ought to have learned enough of my disposition to know that I don't mean everything I say in such things. I only spoke in that manner in order that you might know that I meant what I said when I asked you both to write to me. Our being to each other in the relation of Teacher and pupil may cause some backwardness in writing; but I assure you I would feel very much disappointed if you should not write to me on that account. Enough of this. Suffice it to say "Nance" must write to me, or I will ----- tell "Henry Gates". I suppose your friends and relatives in the Confed. army are in Virginia now if they started at the time you mentioned in your last. I hope they will come somewhere near this place.

I hope to live to receive the ---- promised by you to me. Rest assured that if I live and get to

Georgia I will just so certain as I am now alive come to you all once more. I may be killed, but I will risk it any how. If I go into the battle field. I hope to come out unhurt. We have had several alarms at dead of night since we've been in the army, and I didn't feel the least' excited, although I didn't know whether the enemy were in half a mile of me or not. I hope I may continue as courageous hereafter as there. Give my love to all the family and all my acquaintances & tell them to write to your true friend.

A.B.Spencer

"Camp Gwynn" Portsmouth, Va.
21 Aug. 1861
Dear Friend

A considerable length of time has elapsed since your kind and interesting letter was received; but still I've not answered it, for which heinous offense I must beg your kind forgiveness. I have no excuse whatever to offer. In your last you spoke of your relations leaving for Virginia, and your feelings consequent upon that event; and consequently I concluded to leave you to your own reflections and not harass you with my weak and inefficient sympathy in your behalf. If there is any one quality in which I am more deficient than any other it is that one quality, sympathy. It is true I feel and participate in the joys and woes of others; but I can give more encouragement in the one than in the other, if indeed I can give any in either. I can heartily sympathize with you in all such trials, for I have passed through the same *awful trials;* but I confidentially and sincerely hope one day to receive a blessing that will compensate me one hundred fold more. Many, very many, precious souls have been launched before God's throne since the commencement of the present war; and if the "Abolitionists" still persist in their "hellish" designs, (excuse profanity) there will be many more on both sides; for one is determined to preserve intact the old "Union". Have you ever for a moment considered the disparagement of principles between the two powers; and still it is only a withdrawal of one part of a nation from the other. It is the strangest circumstance I ever noticed in my life. And also notice the difference of principle in the two sections. The one is a marauding, barbarous and confiscating set of villains, the other a magnanimous and civilized people. Just to think of the depredations they have committed upon the fair women and respectable citizens of our beloved country is enough to "chill the blood of age, and make the infant sinews strong as steel". I am very glad indeed to see that the "fair sex" is becoming so *"warlike"*. I have seen a great many notices, in the literary journals, of the ladies forming themselves into military companies in different states. I hope old "Georgia" will not be behind in preparing for an emergency that may happen to our homes in the absence of their protectors. If the women exhibited so much bravery in the "Revolution", why may not those of the present age do the same? Those of the present day are more refined and more sensitive than formerly; consequently it would seem that there would be more bravery in one than in the other. Are there no "Nancy Harts" or "Moll Pitchers" in the Confederacy that would be willing to shoulder the musket or man the

canon? If not, then I will be compelled to acknowledge the
degeneracy of the ladies of this fair land. After making these remarks,
I wouldn't have you for a moment believe that I anticipated any such
contingency, far from it. The "Yankees" will have to kill every man
and boy in the country before such a thing happens, and then I
believe the women would whip them out.

Speaking of patriotism, I must say there is less in this city than
any other of the same size in the "Confederacy". I believe half of its
inhabitants are abolitionists; although there are some as good
southern men, and will fight for our rights as quick as any others; but
the majority is of the "wrong stripe".

Today the band accompanied by three companies belonging to
our Regt. escorted a Virginia Company to the ferry, on their way to
the northern part of this state. They were a nice set of men and had
shown our Regt. a great many favors, we accordingly did this as a
slight requital. I hope it will make a favorable impression among the
women. Tomorrow morning we are requested to attend and perform
at the burial of one of Virginia's sons. Still our Regt. seems to be the
favored of God. We've lost only six or seven men since we've been in
service while the Fourth Geo. Regt. has lost some twenty odd, and at
the present time they have about two hundred on their sick list. Up
to this time no epidemics have made their appearance, and I sincerely
hope will not, for if death must come I prefer it on the battle field, to
death naturally.

Gen. Wool has arrived at Fortress Monroe and "swears
vengeance" against the 2nd Brigade in and around Norfolk. He says
he intends to rase Gasport Navy Yard, and its vicinity to the ground
or compel us to surrender. This he will never do; for each and every
one of us have determined to "do or die." I for one am willing to lose
my life in its defense. If they get possession of this point, we are in a
bad row for stumps. They will then have access to the very heart of
Virginia, as also North Carolina. The only way we can get from this
yard to the ocean is up this river through North C. to Albemarle &
Pamlico Sound. If they should be so fortunate as to get possession

here, I think I shall feel a slight inclination to "get further from here". But enough of war news. I know you will not be interested in it as much so as I and consequently I will stop.

We are about making some arrangements for our winter quarters. I believe the powers "that be" have concluded that it is best for us to construct from logs and clay, rough rude huts for our dens this winter, in preference to being crowded together in the navy yard. I think it is a very wise conclusion. A thousand men being crowded together will necessarily cause a great many diseases that we would otherwise be free from. So you see I will soon be so busy that I will not have time to write you very long letters; and of course will expect you to write to me oftener.

We are about to be provided with a new uniform, of what style or color I know not. In addition to our common dress we will have army overcoats; in fact we will be pretty well *fixed* for a winter campaign. If however we remain in service through the winter, *I* shall be awfully surprised. I think it is impossible for the Lincoln Government to carry on the war so long, without either money or men, neither of which can they get.

You have no idea how much anxiety I have to see *you* all; yet under the present circumstances I would not go back to Georgia if I could, in fact I couldn't if I would. I am getting so well satisfied that this place seems almost like home. If we stay here twelve months longer I am afraid I will be as loath to leave this place as I was to leave Georgia. If I could but see all my friends a little while, and converse with them, I would be contented to stay a good while longer. Still I wouldn't have you to think that I am dissatisfied with my lot. Far from it. I am as well satisfied, and am in as good health as ever before in all my life. I came to be a soldier and am contented with whatever happens to me, considering it all to be my share.

In my last I requested Nancy and Miss Sis to write to me. I hope they will try and gratify me in this simple request, and one being in their power to gratify. It is now getting late, and I am compelled to stop, having to rise very early in the morning. Give my very best respects to all the family, and tell your Father and Nancy to write to me, also the same to all my friends in Dooly.

I remain as ever
Your friend
A.B.Spencer
P.S. Please answer as soon as practicable.
A.B.S.

Diary Entry – 6 September 1861
This morning (6th) being my birthday—21 years old—we bundled up our *trash* and marched to our new encampment, about four miles distant. Quite a novel way in which to celebrate such an occasion. As soon as we arrived, we pitched our tent, and were soon nicely fixed up. About 12 oclock a boat came from Portsmouth, bringing Dr. Morgan having been absent on furlough. By him I rec.d. a letter, and a birthday cake, besides other good things sent me from home. On the (7th) we commenced building another battery, near our first encampment, for the defense of the island. When we first landed we confidently expected to be attacked at every moment. The inhabitants of the island were very much frightened, and some even left the island, for other parts of N. Ca.

Diary Entry - 8 September 1861
This morning (8th) Col. Wright invited us to accompany him across Croatan Sound to the mainland, for selecting a suitable place for a battery. So soon as we landed, we played Dixie, it perhaps the first time it was ever played there. Some of the inhabitants hearing the music were so much frightened, that they even left their houses.

After walking about on the beach some little time, we went to a house not far off, and in it found an old man weighing about two hundred and fifty pounds, and an old woman who said she "wernt afeerd". We then played several other tunes frightening the old man's little dog nearly to death. When we commenced playing, the old man's son "Jake" left for parts unknown, thinking us to be Yankees. The old man was very anxious for "Jake" to hear us, and commenced calling him in most splendid style, "You Jake" "You Jake" was called again and again: but "Jake" didn't make his appearance while we were there. Some ladies next made their appearance: but seemed very much afraid of our instruments. Col. Wright told them "not to be afraid, there was no harm in *those* men", they then came a little nearer.

Diary Entry - 10 September 1861

This morning (10th) Major Lee, in company with a detachment from our Regt. went to Oregon inlet, to get the canon and other implements of war, left at the fort by the North Ca. Soldiers, upon leaving it. Their deserting it was all caused by Capt. Hunter of the Con. Sts. Navy, as grand a coward as ever lived. He almost compelled them to evacuate it, and then published a report that these troops acted cowardly. Major Lee succeeded in saving ten or twelve 32 pounders, and a considerable quantity of shot & shell. This evening a boat came from Norfolk bringing letters and provisions very gladly rec'd.

Diary Entry – 11 September 1861

This morning (11th) hearing the roaring of the surf, we concluded to start for the beach immediately after eating our breakfast. After eating, Doct. Dirk, Fisher and myself started for the Atlantic. We walked three miles across the island to beach of the Sound, and then took passage in a nice little sail boat, to a point on the opposite shore called "Nag's Head", a distance of three miles. On the Sea beach we found a great variety of most beautiful shells. While there I saw the Ocean in all its grandeur. The wind was blowing strong and the waves rolled high upon the beach. After walking about on the beach until we were tired out, we came to the "Hotel de ville" and rested ourselves.

We were soon upon the sound sailing rapidly for our encampment. We arrived just in time to see the Regt. in great excitement, consequent upon hearing that the Federals were on their way to attack Roanoke.

Diary Entry – 12 September 1861
This morning (12th) the band went out in the woods to practice "Smiths March", the first tune I ever learned on a brass instrument. Nothing else of much interest transpired during the day. Col. Wright, upon hearing us play some of our best pieces remarked "that we were making such rapid progress, he would have to leave us here when the Regt. returned to Portsmouth".

Diary Entry – 13 September 1861
Today (13th) a boat arrived from Portsmouth, bringing a dispatch that we were to remain on Roanoke during the winter. I heard a great many remark that they had much rather be confined in the Georgia Penitentiary the same length of time, than on this island. We have now finished another battery mounting twelve guns. These batteries were built under the supervision of Capt. Dimmock of the Engineers' department. He is quite a nice man a perfect gentleman I think.

Diary Entry – 15 September 1861
To-day (15th) Major Lee went to Oregon inlet, to destroy the light house near that place, to prevent the Yankees from coming into the Sound at night. He succeeded in blowing it up, by burying a keg of powder in its' walls, and touching fire to it by a match. It cost the old government some sixty (or) eighty thousand dollars. The glass was an inch or two in thickness. It looked as if it were a pity to destroy such valuable property.

Diary Entry – 16 September 1861

Last night (16th) several rockets and balloons were sent up by the Federals at Hatteras inlet. Again we looked for an attack: but in vain.

"Camp Rescue" Roanoke Island
Currituck Co., North Carolina
September 10th 1861
My dear friend

Since receiving your last most interesting letter, our Regt. has slightly experienced the hardships of a soldier's life. We, the first battalion of our Regt., landed on this island the first of September, and the Second battalion, on the day succeeding. We started from Portsmouth on the 29th of August and travelled about 14 miles on steamboats. The first day and night it rained incessantly and we were compelled to lay down and sleep with our blankets wet, and the next day we dried them in the sun's scorching rays. On our passage we passed through some most beautiful canals. The scenery was the most beautiful I've ever seen. On each side, the canal was covered with the most interesting, soul inspiring shrubbery imagineable. The beautiful windings of the rivers, and their different colored waters all tended to render the scene one of deep interest to those who had never seen such before. The second night we anchored in "Albemarle Sound" and were momentarily expecting to be surrounded and taken prisoners by the "Yankees"; but as "good luck would have it", we escaped such an unpleasant affair. On the lst Sept. after landing, we pitched our tents and remained in that location some five or six days. On the sixth, we marched to our present encampment, a distance of five miles, and by incessant working day and night have nearly succeeded in constructing a most formidable battery. The sixth will always be an era in my earthly career memorable on account of the interesting circumstances connected with it. It being my 21st birthday, and having to march many miles, and being so many miles from home endeavoring to drive from our soil the hireling hordes (of the north?) all render it an epoch in my life never to be forgotten. The island on which we are now situated is rendered famous from several circumstances. During the war a great many years ago, Sir Walter Raleigh landed on this island and had a fierce engagement. It is also noted for being the land where the celebrated "Scuppernong" grape originated. It is about 10 or 15 miles long and from 1 1/2 to 2 1/2 miles wide. There are about five hundred inhabitants, who live principally by fishing. There is one "one horse store", and two very nice churches one Baptist and one Methodist. The inhabitants seem to be very clever, but I believe about half of them are Abolitionists. They, some of them, say we ought not to have come on this island, as they believed the abolitionists would never have bothered them.

I've no doubt it has been reported in Georgia that this Regt. was cut to pieces and taken prisoners. This is altogether a mistake, and I'm happy to inform you of that fact. I haven't much idea that the Yankees will attack this place, if they do; not one will be left to "tell the tale". We have completed one battery and will commence in a few days to build another one. You see they have commenced putting us through now, and to tell you the truth, I'm quite tired of it.

I suppose ere this you've heard of the battle at Hatteras. In it some six or eight hundred of our men were taken prisoners and about ten or fifteen were killed and about the same number were wounded. This battle was the cause of our being ordered to this point. It is reported in camp that after finishing the second battery we will be ordered again to Portsmouth or Savannah, Georgia. Whether this be true or not, I'm unable to say.

We are treated most splendidly by the people of Elizabeth City, and "Edenton", cities of North Carolina. The ladies of the above named places have repeatedly sent us delicacies of almost innumerable variety and last, but not least, was a barrel of fine whiskey, of which I received my proportional share. "I tell you what", we "made it fly". To-day, we received a nice cake sent to us by the ladies of Georgia. It was very thankfully received, as all such things are in Camp life. I have thought once or twice that I would get a furlough and come home to see them all before my time was out; but I've concluded not to come until my 12 months have expired.

In your last you expressed a desire that I would send the family my ambrotype[11]. I would willingly comply; but owing to my present situation I will have to beg your indulgence for a few weeks, that is until I can have it taken, after which time I will most willingly send it. Would it be too much to ask the same favor of you? If not I would be most happy to receive it. If however you think it improper, I shall not be offended; nevertheless, I should like to receive it.

As there is no post office on this island, and we having to send our letters to Portsmouth, by any and every body, we of course can't pay the postage, so if you have to pay any postage upon receiving any of my letters, do not be offended as it is the best I can do. I will give you that unnecessary expense only while we stay on the island, which I hope will not be very long. I haven't received any letters from Samantha yet, but I live in hope, if I die in despair. Give my respects to the family and all inquiring friends, and accept the same for yourself.

I remain your true friend
A.B.Spencer

---

[11] An early type of photograph.

Portsmouth, Va.
Care
Capt. McWhorter
3rd Ga. Regt.
Be certain and give the name of the Regt. in directing the letter.
A,B,S,

Editors Note: This next section, dated September 16, was written as "Cross Writing". Due to the scarcity of paper, after completing the first page, a soldier would turn the paper to a right angle and write a second page on top of the first. This could be hard to read, and even harder to transcribe.

Sept. 16th

You will see by this letter, that it has not been sent at the proper time. The reason why it has not been sent is for want of an opportunity to send it. Nothing of much interest has happened since the preceeding was written; consequently I haven't much of any interest to communicate to you. As to the length of time we expect to remain on the island, I haven't gained much information. It is rumored in the camp among the members of the Regt. that we will probably remain here during the winter. How true this report may be I can not tell; but presume we will return to Portsmouth in a week or so. Col. Wright received a dispatch from our Brigade General, Huges, saying we would return as soon as we had completed the several batteries commenced. This will not be more than two weeks at the farthest. You need not expect to receive many nor very interesting letters from me during our stay at this lonely island. I have the will and desire to write you often; but I haven't the power. There is a general dearth of news here and consequently I haven't much to write that will interest you. Owing to boats not running to and from Norfolk from this place, I have no means of sending to the office as often as I should wish. Rest assured I will write as often as I can and do all in my power to interest you. Yesterday, Sunday as it was, I went in a sail boat to "Nag's Head" a favorite summer resort situated on the beach of the Atlantic, and there I gathered some of the most beautiful shells I have ever seen in my life before. They were scattered over the (beach in profusion?). I intend sending a quantity of them home whenever an opportunity presents itself. If I should be so fortunate as to return home safe and sound I will most certainly take great pleasure in sending you some of them as slight memorials of my high regard. It is true that they are not very valuable; but the circumstances connected with them being gathered render them more precious to me than ten thousand as the same kind gathered by others in such different situations.

While there on the beach the dark (blue?) waves were rolling mountain high and falling upon the shore (&) gave me some slight conception of the horror and beauties of the ocean. A great distance to sea I could plainly see one of old Abe's sail vessels, slowly moving down to Hatteras. On Saturday a large war steamer came very close to the shore, and a man was seen in the rigging, supposed to be making observations upon the shore. I also saw large a very large school of porpoises rolling in the "blue deep". I believe I have nothing else to write. I forgot, I received your father's letter a few days and I will answer it as soon as I can. Give my respects to all inquiring friends. I don't expect you can read this.

Yours etc etc
A.B.Spencer

Diary Entry – 17 September 1861

To-day (17th) a part of our Regt. was detailed to work the guns on the battery first completed.

Forty-five men were also detailed as a Light artillery company, under command of Lieut. Sturgess of the "Burke Guards".

Diary Entry – 20 September 1861

This morning (20) Major Lee and Capt. Hughes started to Norfolk to get some exact information in regard to our stay on the island during the winter. It was said that if Major returned we would certainly remain here. The Regt. has been in great excitement for the past two or three weeks. All afraid to hear from Norfolk, etc. etc. etc.

Diary Entry – 21 September 1861

This morning (21st) early, the eighth N. Ca. Regt. commanded by Col. Shaw, landed on this island. It was then thought to be certain that we would return to Portsmouth soon.

Diary Entry – 22 September 1861

This morning (22nd) two members of the N. Ca. Regt. were buried, having died from taking cold with measles. Soon after eating breakfast this morning, Doct. Dirk, Fisher, Deese, Tillery, Pa and I went again to "Nag's Head" to see the Atlantic. We had quite an interesting time, although it was not so new to us as at first. We, however, gathered more curiosities this time than at first.

Diary Entry – 25 September 1861

Nothing worthy of interest transpired on the (23rd) and (24th). To-day (25th) we had the extreme pleasure of seeing the artilleryman practice shooting at an object placed in the channel of the sound, a distance of three miles. First they fired a blank cartridge from each gun, it being the first time they had ever shot a canon. Next they fired shot and shell at the buoy, and some came very near it particularly the fine 32 pound rifled gun.

Diary Entry – 26 September 1861

To-day (26th) the Sound is completely covered with small steamers, barges, schooners and light boats of every kind. The steamers in the sound are the Raleigh two guns. Curlew two guns.

Diary Entry – 30 September 1861

To-day (30th) we practiced some of our new pieces: but don't make much progress since the departure of Mr. Gorham for Ga. After our practice we drew the provisions we failed to draw several days ago. Among the articles drawn were a quantity of provisions sent us by the ladies of N. Ca.

Diary Entry – 1 October 1861

We neglected to play for the "Guard Mounting" this morning (1st), on account of the sickness of some of the members of the band. It was reported in camp this morning, that a Federal steamer had run aground in Oregon inlet, and immediately the "Dawson Greys", "Governors Guards" and "Athens Guards", were ordered to cook three days provisions. The flying artillery company were also ordered to strike their tents, and bring their guns to this place. They have since arrived, and are now putting their guns aboard a boat to be carried to Oregon. The three companies above mentioned have gone aboard the "Curlew" and "Raleigh".

The "Junaluska" is expected to carry Commodore Lynch. It is also currently rumored that the remainder of the Regt. will follow the above named companies in the morning. Since the above detachment left, we've heard heavy firing in that direction. It, or a part of it, was from our steamers. There were, according to my counting, about twenty guns. -----

The whole camp was alive with joy on account of our glorious victory. Some were so much elated that they had to go and get "tight". And what was worse than all, some of the staff officers were among the number that were guilty of the above act. This moring the Band was requested to play at the burial of a member of the "Portsmouth Rifles:, and we cheerfully consented to grant this simple request. Very unexpectedly to us, they very gentlemanly paid us very handsomely for our trouble. A day or two after this we were invited by Commander Forrest[12] to accompany him on a steamboat excursion down the Elizabeth river.

We went within two miles of "Fortress Monroe" the stronghold of Lincoln's forces. On our passage a gun was fired from the batteries at the "Naval Hospital" to "Craney Island", a distance of four or five miles, and the balls came very near striking our boat. It was fired for the purpose of ascertaining how far this canon would shoot.

The Commadore was accompanied by Genl. Huger, Col. Wright and Col. Blanchard besides other distinguished individuals. He treated the "big bugs" to every luxury he could find; but we poor *devils*, excuse profanity, were offered nothing but old "pop skull" whiskey. The Band has sworn eternal hatred to Commodore Forest. He treated us shamefully, and I may say doggishly. One thing certain he will never get the 3rd Regt. Brass Band to play for *him* again. During my many very many visits to the Navy Yard, I saw a great many interesting sights, and some of a kind to produce quite a ------- ----

This was the last of the diary entries -

"Camp Georgia" 3rd Geo. Regt.
Roanoke Island, N. C.
Nov. 10th 1861
My dear friend

Your kind letter has long since been received; but owing to circumstances beyond my control I have been unable to answer it. I've no doubt you will most willingly excuse me when you know the disadvantages under which I have labored for the past six weeks.

In the first place it was a long time before I entirely "got straight" from our unparalleled hard march after the Yankees on "Chicimocomico"[13] Island. I actually believe some of us will sensibly

---

[12] General Nathan Bedford Forrest, CSA

[13] Often referred to as the "Chicimocomico Races".

feel the effects during the whole of our lives. We had to march 20 miles on the sea beach in sand a foot deep, the first day. We not only marched it, but we run a greater part of the way. At night we slept on the cold sand with no other covering than the blue canopy of heaven. In the morning we found ourselves wet through by the spray from the ocean. We were then compelled to march two or three miles further hoping soon to overtake the Yankees; but alas were most awfully disappointed. I don't think the fastest courser in Georgia could have excelled the speed at which they traveled. When we became satisfied at their superiority in running, we retraced our steps homeward in as quick time as possible.

No sooner had we given up the chase and started on our way back than one of old Abe's war vessels, the Monticello, came as near to the shore as she could with safety and commenced "pouring into our temporary encampment" her fiery shot and shell. I expected every minute to be blown to atoms but providentially none were struck. Some of our men that were behind, stepped out on the beach and shot their rifles at the watchman in the mast. By the manner in which he descended, the ball must have gone very near him. Others planted their flags on the beach bidding defiance to their shot and shell. Some of the solid shot ploughed up the sand the depth of two feet for fifty yards. One of them threw sand all over me and my comrades, although I was not in the thickest part of the engagement. So you see we marched 40 miles during the two days, with nothing to eat but sea biscuit and no water to drink, except that we procured by scratching holes in the marshes, and that salty. We were about four days in this engagement without anything to eat or drink except that procured as above stated. We captured some thirty or forty of their prisoners, and captured their whole store (stores of about 800 or 1,000 men). On board the steamer Fannie, a boat we captured from the Yankees, there were one thousand and forty five blue overcoats for the Yankees. They, the coats, have been distributed among the members of the Regt. Each one of the band procured one and we now look quite grand. After returning from this trip we were told that we would soon return to Portsmouth. We were kept in this suspense for a long time when we were told that the War Department had decided that we must stay on this island so long as the Yankees remained at Hatteras. We were ordered to clear up a camp for winter quarters. We have been busily engaged in this work for two or three weeks, in fact ever since I received your last letter. For these reasons I've not answered your letter until now, and if it were not Sunday I wouldn't have time now. From these reasons I think you will certainly excuse me, promising to do better next time.

The past week I've been busily engaged working on our winter cabin. Ours is a double log cabin, each room 12 by 18 feet and a passage 6 feet wide between. We have built it up ready for covering, and will finish it next week. There are ten of us at work on the house. There are two of our Band absent at Portsmouth. They will return sometime next week I hope. So you see we will then have 12 in our house, 6 in each room.

It is now pretty cold weather, and we need our winter houses very bad. We have had some pretty heavy frosts for the past week or two, and it is still growing colder every day. We have plenty of shingles and lumber of every kind and everything necessary for building purposes.

Yesterday morning our gunboats returned, having been absent some two or three weeks. In passing Hatteras they saw a vessel stranded on the bar. They immediately run up for rescuing the crew. They found it to be a French sloop of war carrying 6 guns. They saved the crew consisting of 140 men and then set fire to the vessel. In passing through "Ocracoke" inlet, one of our boats, the steamer "Winslow" accidentally run against an anchor that had been sunk, for filling up the channel, and tore a hole in her hull, causing her to sink almost immediately. Everything on board, except the engine, was saved before she was entirely gone. The Commander of the French sloop of war remarked to Commodore Lynch (of our boats) that notwithstanding we had lost the Winslow, we had gained much more by rescuing them from a watery grave, intimating that we would gain favor with the French government. They passed here a day or so since "en route" from Norfolk, I hear so many reports in camp now days I can't tell what to believe. I will give you some as reports and not as truth. It is currently rumored in our camp that eight thousand N. C. troops are ordered to report to Col. Wright on this island next Tuesday morning. I think this is true. I can't tell what it is for. Some of the knowing ones however say that we meditate an attack on the Yankees at Hatteras. Others say the Yankees contemplate a simultaneous attack on Norfolk and Wilmington, N. C., and that our Regt. will be removed to one of the two places. I almost pray that the latter report is true. Anything now to get off this island. I am willing to go almost anywhere else except stay here.

We seldom get any mail, and have no chance to send off any of our letters. And we have to work so hard during the day that we are so tired at night we care about nothing but sleeping. While we were stationed at Portsmouth we had some accommodations; but since we've been here we've had none whatever. We have plenty to eat, such as it is. Beef, bacon, sea bread, and flour and occasionally we have a few eggs, wild ducks, and geese; but only occasionally we have a chance to buy such things. If we were at Portsmouth we could almost live on oysters. I do hope we will return soon.

The health of our Regt. is very good now. The North Carolina Regt. has lost some twenty odd men since they've been on the island, the disease was measles. I believe measles and mumps have gone through our Regt. I have escaped everything of the kind so far. I have been sick two days only since I left home, and hope I will continue to be so healthy throughout the campaign.

---- whole mess has been quite healthy. None have been sick more than two or three days at a time.

I am very sorry indeed to hear that the health of the D.L.I. is so bad. I knew some of those that died in Virginia. Peace to their ashes. They died in a noble and just cause and I've no doubt their names will be remembered as martyrs to the cause of Liberty and Independence. I wish you could have seen some of the Yankee letters we found at Hatteras. They represented themselves as fighting for their flag. Some say they were forced into it, others that they were fooled into it. I found a great many envelopes with the strangest pictures painted on them imaginable. I hope some day to have an opportunity of showing them to you. I have no doubt howeverbut that Mat Poole (sure enough) has shown you some of them as I doubt her brother has sent her some of them. I have several things I took from them besides others I've sent home. I have a snuff box I think will suit you and *Aunt Nancy* to keep tooth powders in. You have no idea how many times I think of you all in Dooly. Sometimes I can hardly tell which I should rather see, you all or my own family; but if I didn't want to see my mother and sister worse I should consider myself devoid of all parental affections. I assure you however that the people of Dooly however are next in my heart. For the kindness received while there, I never can sufficiently repay you. I assure you however you have my heartfelt thanks. If God spares my life, I will most certainly come back to see you all so soon as my time expires. I should like very much to teach for you all again; but I've no doubt you will have procured a teacher that will give better satisfaction before I return. If I do teach for you any more I will have to board with your Father. I will promise not to leave until he drives me away. I will put your family to as little trouble as possible and consider myself as one of the family, to come when called and go when bid. Besides all this, *Robert and I will plough*. As for Samantha writing to me I have long since despaired. If she only knew what pleasure letters afforded me, out of the world as I am, she would be sure to write to me. Seeing what fate the letters of the "Yankees" met with, I have concluded to burn all my letters, so if I am taken prisoner they will get none of mine to read. I hope you will think I act wisely in so doing. If it were not for this I wouldn't treat your letters with such disrespect. I have been keeping a diary ever since I've been in service, and maybe I will let you read it when I return. I don't know when I'll be able to send this off, but will do so as soon as possible. Give my respects to all the family and Sis, too, excuse me I mean Miss Louisa.

Give my respects to everybody. Write soon. I remain your true friend.

A.B.Spencer
3rd Regt. Geo. Vols.
Portsmouth Va.
Care Capt. McWhorter
D. Greys

Portsmouth, Virginia
December 1861
My dear friend

Your kind letter reached me long since, but for reasons I shall afterwards name I have neglected it until the present moment. In the first place, after reaching this place, from that detestable island Roanoke, I was necessarily very much confused and fatigued. I hadn't seen any ladies in so long a time I was compelled to go and see them. Besides we had to clear up another camp, *as we are so fond of it.*

You spoke something of the approach of Christmas and of the manner in which you spent it last and how you expected to spend it this time. It is true, I expect, that you never spent such a dull one before; but how great a difference it has been with me. I never in my life before was absent from home on Christmas, and of course you can imagine my feelings on that day. The ladies of this place have an institution they call the "Ladies Feast". To gain admittance into this place you pay the *enormous* sum of ten cents. If you wish supper, the pay is *smaller* 50 cents. While eating you are attended by most *beautiful* ladies. Isn't that glorious? I have attended two nights and expect to do so several times more. Last night I escorted Miss Lane to the feast. "She is a perfect beauty, very much like M-M-M –M–". When you come to the line previous to this, you must not think any for fear you might come to the wrong conclusion, as to whom I mean by M - . I know exactly how you will decide it but I will not deny it as I know you won't believe me. I will simply say there are more ladies than one whose name commences with M. There were a great many pretty ladies present; but I must say that old Georgia beats all others in this respect, if not in others. I have not seen one that will compare with those in my native state. They may all be "well meaning"; but they are mortal ugly. Miss Mat Poole's brother left this place for Georgia a few days since, probably you may see him.

Miss Mag I am almost ashamed to send you such poor letters as I do. I am in camp a greater part of my time and of course my mind can't possibly be engaged on any one object for any length of time. At this very moment, I hear one of the boys of the Reg. attempting to speak, others are "*carrying* on" in some other way, and this is the way nearly all the time night and day; and it is impossible for my letters to be of any interest to you, receiving as you do, such interesting ones from Miss *Mat*.

In a day or so we will commence building our winter quarters. I do think it is too hard for us to build winter quarters for others, just as able to do it as we are. If we do under-go hardships, it is a consolidation to know that we have the sympathy of those at home. If it were not for the ladies, a great many of our brave soldiers would suffer. I never knew what it was to be absent from a mother so long a time, twelve months. But, notwithstanding all these inconveniences, I know that I am conferring a blessing on her, in guiding my comrades to prevent our glorious country from being overrun by the hireling slaves of the north. I know too that I will receive a Mother's blessing if we should gain our independence. If I could always serve under as efficient officers as ours, I should be contented to stay in service for three years if necessary. I think we will certainly lose our Col.

There has been a petition from the Georgia legislature to have Col. Wright appointed Brigadier General of the forces on the coast of Georgia, and I think it is pretty generally believed that this petition will be granted. Col. Wright is fully competent to fill this office, and he deserves promotion; and on his account I do hope he may be so promoted, although I hate very much to lose him. If we could only (be) transferred with him to the coast it would be glorious; but it is no use thinking about that, notwithstanding such has been the rumor in our camp for a long time. I think we are just as near Georgia now as we will be before our time of enlistment expires. I expect when our time expires we will be requested again to enlist for the war, If necessary, I expect to reenlist. I know that if the war does continue I will be needed much more where I now am than at home, and of course I shall go where I am most needed.

It would be a great pleasure to me, you know, to stay in Georgia at any time, but you know too it would be a stigma on my name to do as your bird does; that all would fail to erase from the tablets. I suppose you are fully aware of the bird I mean, if not, I will let you remain in ignorance, as "ignorance is bliss". It may be that he enjoys himself finely; but if I were to do that way, I should always consider myself an outcast from society, and never expect any more enjoyment on earth. I don't wish you to say anything about this. It might cause unpleasant feelings to arise.

Some time ago, you know that I promised to send my ambrotype so soon as I could have one taken. I will send it at the earliest opportunity. I would that I could send you something more acceptable; but as long as you have requested it, I comply hoping you will see in it your sincere well wishes. I consider myself highly honored and hope some day, not far distant, to repay you in some feeble way. It will be a great pleasure, to me to know, though absent far away, that there are still some who will sometimes think of him whose endeavor it has always been to please those with whom he has been associated.

On our arrival at this place, we met with a grand reception. Everyone seemed to be very much elated at our return, and everywhere saluted us by waving their handkerchiefs, and honoring us with their pleasant smiles. We were met by the 22nd Ga. Regt. and two Va. Cavalry companies. Gen. Blanchard complimented us very highly by stating "that he felt as if he had regained his strength." As all are a little fond of flattery, you can imagine how we received it. I am truly glad that we have once more returned to a civilized country. We feel now as if we had something to contend for.

While on Roanoke, we had no place to enjoy ourselves. We were compelled to wear out the monotony, in ---- we can sometimes go to town, and enjoy ourselves a little. Besides all, since we've arrived at this place we have received our pay. While on Roanoke, we were out of money all the time, consequently we were without any source of enjoyment whatever. Until now I never before knew the wickedness carried on in camp, gambling and drinking are carried to an alarming excess indeed. Yesterday I saw men intoxicated, and gambling I never dreamed were guilty of such things. Although I say that I have done neither, it is nevertheless true. The temptations are strong; yet a great many are overcome by them. I have spoken to some of my most intimate friends of the danger and error of their course; but they all say they were unconsciously led into it by others. Men who were at home considered gentlemen have now become arrant thieves. I do hope this war will soon come to a close.

This morning I have determined to stay in camp awhile, to see if I can possibly restore the equilibrium of my mind. I hope, the next time I hear from you, I shall receive an interesting account of the manner in which you spent Christmas. I have, as near as I can, given you some little idea of how I spent mine. It is not to be supposed that one in my situation could enjoy himself as well as I have for the past day or two. Wouldn't I have had a "gay time" if I had remained (on) Roanoke dreaming myself to death about the unpleasantness of my lot. The only objection I have to this place is that we have to cook for ourselves, and sleep on the cold, cold ground. I hope soon to sleep in our house we intend to build, and then I will be as rich as any one could well wish.

I have just learned that a member of my company expired this morning at ten oclock. This is the first time we've been called on to mourn the loss of a single man since we've been in service, while nearly all the other companies have lost one or more. Our Capt. will send his corpse home to be buried by his friends. He was a poor man and leaves a large family in a destitute condition to mourn his loss. I am not afraid of their suffering so long as we have such brave women at home to supply their wants. The members of the company will pay all expenses of transportation etc., and accordingly a subscription has been taken up for that purpose. Soldiers are much more liberal than one would suppose they could be with such small pay. In fact, they are too much so for their own good. Only one of our company will be allowed to accompany the corpse home. I did think that Genl. Blanchard acted wrong in not letting more leave; but under the present excitement as regards an attack on the place, I think he acted right. Some think that there will be an attack in this place in a short time; but I can't see any more signs of one now than I did months ago. I think it is more smoke than fire.

I am very glad indeed to know that Jack has recovered from his long sickness; and that he feels so much interest in his company as to "stick to it through thick and thin". I have determined to be discharged only when I am necessarily compelled. I am sorry to say however that there are several of my immediate acquaintance which have taken advantage of this, simply to be released from service. Our time of enlistment is fast drawing to a close, and I can't but thank the overruling providence for preserving me through so many dangers and difficulties. I consider it a special dispensation of providence in keeping us from being destroyed by the shells of the Yankees on Chicimocomico Island. The iron hail fell and fast around us; yet not a man was killed and but very few were even touched. I don't know how soon we may be called upon to face the enemy upon the field of battle; but come when it may, we are ready to give them a grand reception. Some brave heart is sure to fall; but even that is small in comparison to the rescuing of so many brave and fair women from the clutches of such base hirelings.

On the morning of the 22nd ultimo[14] there was a skirmish at "Newport News" between the Confederates and Federals. The disasters on either side I haven't learned. This morning there has been heavy firing down the river towards James River, supposed to be an engagement between the Confederate steamer "Patrick Henry"

---

[14] Ultimo, or "ult" meaning the last date listed prior to the current date.

and the blockading vessel at the mouth of the above named river. We will probably receive some account of it tomorrow's paper.

I suppose ere this you've heard something about the great iron floating steam battery "Merrimac", being constructed in the Navy Yard. It is a most formidable affair, and when it does go out you will hear a very favorable account of it. It carries 12 guns of largest calibre, the whole encased with timber one foot thick, and this with wrought iron four inches thick. There has been a proclamation issued to allow those enlisting to be absent home on a six weeks furlough. Some of this Regt. have enlisted. It will probably be finished in six or eight weeks, if nothing happens to prevent it. To show (how) much it is dreaded by the Yankees, it is only necessary to state the fact, that the Lincoln government has offered a million of dollars for its destruction. The day we arrived at this place, two men were arrested suspicioned of attempting to burn the Navy Yard, and the iron battery. They are now in safe custody on the old man of war "United States". They will be severely punished, if any proof can be found which to convict them. This battery is expected to operate in the waters between this place and Chesapeake bay. The defenses of this place are now such as to render the capture of this place impossible. The batteries at "Craney Island", 2 miles distant from this place are now being made bombproof, to prevent an accident similar to that at "Port Royal" S.C. I think after all the fuss about the "Port Royal " affair it will result in good to the Southern Confederacy. Col. Wright has just come into camp bringing the news that Commodore Lynch had taken the steamer "Sea Bird" down below Craney Island, and with (it) had captured a Yankee schooner. This was the cause of all the firing heard this morning.

I shall expect a long answer to this soon, by return mail. You can't imagine what a pleasure it is to me to receive those long, long letters. I wouldn't get tired of reading them even if they occupied a week, to glance over them. Whether mine are interesting or not, I am unable to say. I am inclined to think they are not however. I endeavor, however, to do the best the circumstances allow. "Angels could, no more". I wish you a happy, happy New Year. My respects to Miss Sis and all your family. I shall expect an answer from Miss Samantha soon.

I remain as ever your affectionate friend,
A.B.Spencer

CHAPTER TWO

1862

After the Battle of Malvern Hill, on July 2, 1862, groups of Confederate soldiers spent a cold day in the drizzeling rain buring their dead. The battle was so intense and disturbing to Maj. Gen. John B. Magruder that he put in for a transfer to a unit less likely to see such fighting. General Robert E. Lee honored his request and relieved him of all duties with the Army of Northern Virginia. It was widely speculated that Magruder was drunk on duty during the battle. Alva mentions this in a letter in this chapter, identifying Magruder by name. Magruder himself was partially to blame for this, due to his reputation as a heavy handed drinker. However, Gen. Lee never pursued these charges due to a lack of witnesses willing to come forward. Alva's only mention of the battle at Sharpsburg, Maryland, is that his knapsack was stolen there and he lost everything he had. Fredericksburg made for a cold December. Many suffered at the hands of "Old Man Winter" in the form of frostbitten limbs. Wood was scarce, clothing was sparse, many a corpse was releived of the valuable clothing he no longer needed. Alva dosen't comment on the actual battle, but the hardship of the bitter cold, the hunger, and the embarassment and shame of having to "steal" clothing from the dead Yankees to survive.

From across the Atlantic we read:

"What is it that makes a people so small in number to sustain so great an effort? There is but one source of such strength as this that recruits such armies without bounty or pay,-a sense of right, a knowledge that their cause is just. The people of the south are called "rebels;" it just because they are not rebels that they have this strength. ------ The people of Western Virginia have rebelled against the lawful authorities of their state. They are the only body of rebels; and, strange to say, they are on the side of the north."

The Times of London, July 17, 1862

This letter was written by Thomas J. Cone (Margaret L. Cone's brother) to his father William B. Cone. Thomas and his brother Andrew Jackson Cone, both served in the 18th Georgia, Co. I.

Dumfries, Va.
January the 1, 1862
W. B. Cone
Dear Father,
Your kind letter which was dated the 18th of last month was duly received Dec. the 30. You can't imagine with how much pleasure it was perused and the good news that it brought that all were injoying good health affords me much pleasure, but I was sorry to here that ant Nancy was sick. I would have answered your letter before now, but I thought that I would wait until the first of January and I would draw my money and send it home but I here now that we will not draw any money until the first of next month. As soon as I get it will send it home. You said in your letter that Jack and Mr. Johnson would be here by the first of January, but they have not come back yet. Pa I expect it is a good idea to send somebody with him. I will tell you circumstance that happened about----
About a week before Christmas this regiment started ten men 1 from every company to Richmond after a wagon. Armstrong appointed William Rodgers. And when he had got back to Fedrickburg next morning. Next morning all fixed up their teems and Rogers was missing and his two coats was found in his wagon and blanket and they have been sent to the company. It is thought that he

is killed though we do not know it. Armstrong had gone in to see what is the matter and he has not come back yet. We are fearful that he is killed but we hope not. There is a considerable excitement in camps at this time. General Whitin commanded us to keep one day's rations cooked a head. And we are expecting to have to fall into a line of battle pretty soon. We cant stay here much longer without a fight I don't think. All the boys are anxious to meet the Yankees. I have nothing new the write to you. I would have liked verry well to have been at ----

Give my love to all of the family and except of the a father, I remain your obedient son until death.

Thos. J. Cone

P.S. I sent you 20,00 dolars by Sam Ivey let me know when you get it.

T.J.C.

Another letter written by Thomas, this time to his sister Margaret.

Dumfries Va. Jan. 7th 1862
Miss M. L. Cone
Dear Sister
I seet myself this morning to let you know how we are getting along at this time. Jack arrived from home at last, on the fifth of this month. He has been in verry good health since he came. I can tell you we were verry glad to see him. He was on the road five days and said he had no trouble at all. He had to leave his trunk at Brookses Station as he had no way to bring. At Brookses Station he hierd a horse to dumfries and then he had but two miles to walk. I have not said anything about my health yet. It has been three weeks since I have done any duty at all though I have not been confined to my bed at all. About three weeks ago I was taken with the mumps. After I got well of them, I was taken with the feaver which lasted me three or

four days. After this I was takened with the yellow jaundice and have got them yet. I feel much better today and I think that I will survive them all. At least I hope so. I(t) is verry cold wether here at this time. The ground has been covered with snow ever since the first day of January. The Potomac was about half frosed over the other day. Jack says he does not like this part of the world much. We have been looking for a fight for the last ten days but it has not com yet, and I dont think it will.

You must tell Ma that I am a thousand times oblige to her for my new suit for nothing could have been more exceptable with me. But tell Ma I am afraid she is doing two much. We would ask nothing else of her for we have got more than we can toat. Jack[1] was verry muched at our houses, when I got here, he said to some of the boys, "what negro house will I stay in". Jack surprise a great many of the company as none of them thought that he would never come back. I have herd Sient Carter say that he thought that Jack was goin to play Tom Collier[2] on us, but thank god he was disappointed. Siss you never say anything about Granma. You must let me know how she is getting along and give her my best respects. Als let me know how every body is getting along. Jack told me you all was well and that was about all he has said about home. I have nothing of importance to write so I must bring my foolishness to a close. You must excuse bad writing and spelling for I am in a hirry. Give my best respects to Pa Ma and all the rest of the family and except of the same yourself. I remain your brother until death.

Thomas J. Cone

---

[1] Andrew Jackson Cone. Thomas Cone and Margaret Lucinda Cone's brother. A.J. Cone of the 18th GA., Co I.

[2] Tom Collier, 18th GA., Co. I.

South Mills N.C.

Feby. 17th 1862

Dear Friend

Yours of a late date was received not long since, and would have been answered long since, but for reasons I shall afterwards mention. I've no doubt, but that ere this you've heard of the capture of Roanoke Island. The enemy over-powered our men, and of course after contesting awhile they were obliged to surrender. From all the information I can gather I can't believe the men on the island fought bravely. The number of killed and wounded on either side we are unable to learn. During the engagement at the island, our gunboats, (8) in number, got out of ammunition, and withdrew to Elizabeth City to procure a supply. While our boats were absent, the enemy got possession of the island, and they remained at the city. On Monday morning our boats were attacked by an overpowering number of Federal vessels. They fought as long as they could, and then tried to make their escape to this place, on the Dismal Swamp Canal, three got here safe. Out of the (8) boats that we had in the engagement, (3) were saved, (1) captured by the Yankees, and the rest were burnt and sunk. Upon reception of this news (5) companies of our Reqt. under Major Lee's command was ordered to this place. They arrived at this place on Monday night, the very time I received your last. During Monday night the Lt. Col. Reid rec'd. orders to come on immediately with the remainder of our Regt. We were accordingly ordered to cook all the provisions that we had, preparatory to leaving in the morning, to rejoin the remaining companies of our Regt. We started at (8) oclock in the morning, and arrived at South Mills, (10) oclock at night, a distance of (30) miles. This is what I call a "force march" don't you? Not having any tents, we were quartered in the churches, academies, stables, mills, etc. I am staying with Mr. Cherry, a fine gentleman. The Yankee gunboats are lying off Eliz. City all the while. The other day Col. Wright took two or three companies from our Regt. to the city. While there he went to the wharf, and waved the Confederate flag at the Yankees daring them to come ashore; but they seemed to have no such inclination. On the 14th Lt. Col. Reid went on board the Yankee boat under flag of truce to make some arrangements for exchange of prisoners. He reported that several of the boats had holes through them. So it seems that some of our shots took effect. I don't suppose we will ever receive a correct account of the number killed and wounded in this battle. As to our having a fight here I think it is altogether improbable. They are afraid to come on land they *know* we can whip them. All the men that were captured on our boats have been released on parole of honor. It is supposed by some that those captured on the island would be released, this I hardly believe. If we had been on Roanoke we might have shared the same fate; but I think we would have fought a good long time before surrendering. Now between you and I, the North Carolina boys won't fight.

In your last you wished me a "knapsack full of Valentines", I wish I could have been in Portsmouth, probably I *would* have rec'd them. At the same time, I don't want you to believe for a moment that I would look for one from a Va. woman, quicker than I would from a Ga. *lady*, far from it. If certain things hadn't transpired, I wouldn't have been surprised if *somebody* had received a Valentine from one in the 3rd Ga.___ . The blame all rests on the Yankees, *you* must blame *them*, and not m-m-somebodyelse.

I wanted to have sent some but unfortunately was ordered away on the 12th. If it hadn't been for this, I should have sent several. In reference to that Virginia lady you were speaking about, I am sorry you should think me so fickle as to change one Ga. for a Va. lady. I must acknowledge that she is a *very* pretty woman, calculated to captivate almost any one; but I'm not quite gone yet. As to her patriotism I'm unable to say. There are so many unsound in Portsmouth and Norfolk, I can't tell "tother from which". Now between you and I, the reason I visit these ladies, is to try and wear away some of the dull monotony of camp life.

I am very glad that my old patrons have secured the services of another teacher. It is impossible for me to tell when I shall return. If I ever return, I pledge my sacred honor, to come and see those who have shown for me such pure friendship. Sometimes I am almost compelled to give up; but I'm constantly buoyed up with the hope of receiving the smiles of approving friends. But for the circumstances in which I'm placed, I would write more. Give love to the family and Miss Sis. I am as ever your true friend.

A. B. Spencer
Portsmouth Va.
Co. C. 3rd Ga.reg
P.S. Direct letters
as before. ABS

Portsmouth, Virginia
May 4th 1862
Dear

Your kind and very interesting letter was rec'd. a few days since. It must have been delayed a long time, as it was dated (9th Apl.) and arrived 2nd May. I had almost despaired of ever hearing from you again. It has been almost a month since I heard from you or Miss Mance. I attribute the long delay to the postal department and not to you.

I suppose that ere this you have received intelligence of our recent engagement near South Mills N.C. On the morning of the 19th of April, the enemy landed in Camden Co. N.C. 10 or 15 miles from South Mills. Immediately upon the reception of this intelligence, Col. Wright ordered, 6 companies belonging to our Regt. and 3 pieces artillery to a place called "Sawyer's Lane", there to await the approach of the enemy. About 12 the enemy made his appearance. As soon as they were seen, the Artiller opened fire (on) them, causing them to get into the woods for protection. The artillery kept up this firing for two hours, the enemy replying. Not one of our men was injured by their cannon. About 3 in the evening we saw the enemy marching towards in large force. The engagement soon commenced, the bullets and shell flying around us like hail. The force of the enemy was estimated at 5 or 6 thousand ours 300. Notwithstanding this overwhelming odds, we repulsed them several times, strewing the field with the dead and wounded. Seeing we were overpowered Col. Wright gave the order to retreat, and by that means we were saved from being captured. Our loss is 6 killed 15 wounded 3 or 4 taken prisoners. The Federal loss is 3 or 4 hundred killed 25 or 30 prisoners and a great many wounded. The enemy left on the battle field 100 guns, 1100 lbs. powder, knapsacks, canteens, etc. in abundance. One thousand yards of submarine telegraph cable was found on the battle field, with which they held communication with their gun boats during the engagement. During the engagement a minnie ball struck my left hand mutilating one of my fingers a good deal. My little finger and the one next it were both somewhat injured. On account of this wound I have been unable to perform any duty since the 19th. At first it was thought that my finger would be amputated; but as yet it hasn't been done. I am staying in a private family, and am very well treated indeed. I hope my hand will be well in two or three weeks.

We have had quite a reorganization in our Regt. Col. Wright was reelected & Col. Reid. Others not. The Dawson Greys have an entirely new set of officers. Capt. McWhorter was not elected. Lt. Geer is now our Capt. By the conscription bill[3], all the twelve month troops are retained in service for two years to come. I don't expect to see you all soon perhaps never again. It is now reported that Portsmouth and Norfolk are to be evacuated. I give this only as a report. An engagement is daily looked for at Yorktown. The Merrimac is lying out in the river ready to leave at any moment. If these two cities are evacuated the Merrimac will be their only protection. Another engagement is expected at South Mills soon I hope so at least.

I should have been very much pleased to have been with you fishing. I know I should have enjoyed myself finely; but such pleasures needn't be anticipated yet awhile. I can't for my life

---

[3] Conscription Bill – April 1862, the Confederate draft.

imagine, the sender of that Valentine, unless it be some one in the Pulaski Vols. I think you ought to tell me that joke on Mance as she told on you. Tell her there is no time to be sick now, she must be cheerful, and we will them out soon don't you believe so?

Pa is with me yet; but by the recent law, he will leave for home soon. I hate very much to see him leave I assure you. I know I shall be very lonesome and dull. As I can use only one hand I *know* you will excuse this scribbling. Don't wait long before you answer this as I'm awful blue. Give my love to the family and all enquiring friends.

As ever your affectionate friend.

A.B.S.

Penfield Geo.
May 14th 1862
My dear friend
You will see by the caption of this letter that I am once more at my native town enjoying the pleasures of home. Col. Wright seeing that I was unable to follow my Regt. kindly gave me permission to go home, and return so soon as I might be able. I arrived here last Saturday, greatly surprising everybody. I found everything had undergone a considerable change in the past twelve months. Our town is almost deserted, some ten or twelve of the largest houses are now vacant.

I suppose ere this you've heard of the evacuation of Portsmouth and Norfolk. Nearly all the Government stores had been removed previous to its evacuation. Since I left, the Merrimac has been blown to atoms. The commanders attempted to carry her to Richmond, but finding it impossible, they blew her all to pieces. I think the iron and guns were all taken off before she was destroyed. It is a great loss; but it couldn't be avoided. The one, that was being built in the Navy yard, has been removed to Richmond, there to be finished. The enemy, so soon as they heard of the two cities being evacuated, landed at "Ocean View" and marching to the two towns, took possession. I do hope our winter quarters were destroyed; I do think it very hard, to build them two encampments, don't you?

Where our Regt. now is I have no idea; but suppose it--is somewhere between Portsmouth and Weldon. It was reported, in our camp before I left, that we would join Jackson's command in N. Western Va. I think we will have pretty hard times now, much more so than heretofore.

In my last, I very impertinently addressed you in a style, which I had no right to use. I am truly ashamed of myself, I hope you will excuse me when I tell you it was entirely unintentional. I will be more careful next time.

I shall remain home until I get entirely well. I am getting along pretty well now, and hope to be well in two or three weeks. If possible, I will try and come and see you; if I do not, you may rest assured, it is because I was unable.

You must write oftener now as I have come nearer to you. Give my respects to the family and all others of my acquaintance.

I remain as ever your true friend.

A B. Spencer
Paper is scarce.

At home Penfield Ga.
June 2nd 1862
My dear friend

Yours of a recent date was rec'd. not long since, but for my absence from home. I reckon you think that if I could go away from home any where I could certainly come to Dooly. I will try and explain how I came to be absent. Soon after I arrived here, my Aunt and two cousins came down from Covington to see me. While here they begged Ma so much that she was compelled to let me go. I was absent only *one* week. While there I enjoyed myself very much indeed.

You will have seen, after reading this letter, that there is but little or nothing to write about from this place. I would that I could write something to interest you but I do the best I can, and the poet says "Who does the best he can, does well, acts nobly; angels could no more". There are no young men here, or rather very few. I enjoy myself very much with the girls; but you know I can't be with them all the time, so I'm sometimes a little dull, or to use a more common expression, "I have the blues". I know you can sympathize with me in that, as you say you've been afflicted with it, and of course know how disagreeable it is.

Yesterday we rec'd a letter from Pa stating that the 3rd Geo. had gone to Rich. He was unable to go, having a very severe cough. He seemed to look for warm work soon. We are looking every day to hear a bloody battle near Richmond. Our troops seem confident of success. I do *hope* it may be so. Enclosed in Pa's letter was yours and Mance's letters of the 14th ult. I know you will be somewhat relieved as you expressed a fear that they fall into the hands of the Yankees.

Miss Margaret I have made you a promise, and that in all sincerity. I fully intended to keep it; but I fear I will be unable to do so. When I promised you to come and see you if ever I came home, I never dreamed it would be under such circumstances as I'm now placed. In the first, Ma objects, saying that I haven't long to remain at home, and she wishes me to be with her as much as possible. I know you will be disappointed, but not more so than myself. I had made my arrangements to come; but under present circumstances it is next to impossibility. I know you will hereafter look upon my promises as false; but before passing judgement upon me please reflect for one moment that I act simply from a Mother's request. I will try and redeem myself some day. Full well I recollect another promise unfilled. I promised to send you my ambrotype, and haven't done it. This one I will fulfill, if I'm spared. I will send it to you before I leave if possible. I don't expect you will believe it until you see it.

I am now very busy preparing myself to start again for the field of action. I honestly had rather be in service than remain at home. I am so used to a crowd I hardly know how to content myself. If I go to church I see nothing but ladies, if I go down town I see nothing but old men; so I just set at home and read nearly all the time.

Tell *Aunt* Nancy I haven't forgotten her yet. Every time I send love to the *family*, I include hers and Mrs. Grahams'. If I don't mention her name, she may always know she is not forgotten by the "Snuff box finder". Tell Mance I will write to her in a few days. Give my love to your Father, Mother, Mance, Miss Nancy, Eliza, Babe, Louisa, Miss Sis, and everybody else in the neighborhood.

A.B.S.

Written by Thomas J. Cone to his sister Margaret. Thomas is listed on the 18th GA, Co I, Roster as having died in the war at the Battle of Gaines Mill, which was 27 June 1862. Family records however list his date of death as 8 July 1862. It's possible that the family didn't receive word of his death until the 8th of July. This letter was written just six days before his death.

Federickshall, Va.
June the 21, 1862
Miss M. L. Cone
My Dear Sister:
I once more have a chance to let you know how we are getting along. I am more than glad to say to you that we are doing tolerably well. I and Jack are both harty. I am sure we never had better health in our lives. I will first tell you the health of our comp. R. B. Cone, Jr., bill Uncle Jim is well and harty. John & Roberts and several of the boys that you are not acquainted with, was left in Richmond. But all of them came in yesterday but John & Roberts. P--- I will tell you the truth. I am afraid John will never stand a camp life. I will tell you just how he is. When he is in camps he dwindles away every day until he is sent to the hospitle and as soon as he gets there he fattens every day. He always leaves the hospitle too soon. So he has used himself so that he has never got over that spell he had last fall. You would

hardley know him his mind is injured and he is not like the same man, besides he is verry careless. His stomach is week and when he comes to the camps he eats to much and soon becomes puny again. When I left him last, which was on the llth of this month, I give him 20 dollars and told him to go to a private house & told him not to come to us again until he got well and sound. He was not sick much he only had the dirareah which troubles him a great -eal. Now I will tell you something about our movements for the last ten days. We let Richmond on the 12 to reinforce Stonewall Jackson who was at Winchester. We takened the cars and come to Lynchburg and stoped three days, at which time Gen. Sawdens brigade come in from Savanah Ga. So I struck up with the 13th Ga. Regt. and found Sa Mobley and I can tell you there was all rejoicing. So we started------ for Centervill and got in -wenty miles of the place and met Jackson's army coming back. So we came back twenty miles on foot and taken the train and arrived at this place yestarday which is fifty miles above Richmond on the Central railroad. So you see that all of Jacksons armey has left the valey. So you see we have two hundred and fifty thousand troops around Richmond and the furthest ones off is 50 miles. I can't tell you what they mean. I thought they will make McClelland hunt for the Potomac, pretty soon. We here today that there will be no more hostilities in sixty days, if -his be so we will get (to) come home, but I am afraid it is not so.

I have been looking for Pa every day for ten days. I am about to give him out. I written to him while I was in Lynchburg not to come for I did not know where we would go to, and am in the same fix yet. There is a great -eal talk of peace here now since England has recognized our independence. It is thought that Lynchburg will make one more effort and that will be to get Richmond. Our boys is not half so anxious to get into a fight as they were. We have never got the chance to shoot a Yankee but we have seen all seens that can be seen on a battle field. The boys are all anxious for Pa to come as they have several Yankee's tricks (trinkets) they want to send home. I got several things myself. I got me a sword and several other little things.

In one of the Yankees knapsacks I found a beautiful Yankee's girl's picture. This is all that I have time to write. If I had time I could write all day. I have forgot to say one thing.

This day twelve monts ago we was mustered in survice.

We will try to come home as soon as we can and If I ever get there I will tell you what home is. Write soon and direct your letter to Richmond. Give my love to everybody especially to Pa & Ma and my kinfolks and except of the same yourself.

Excuse bad writing and spelling. I remain your Brother until death.

Thos. J. Cone

P.S. Tell Miss Marcy & Betty I have treated them mean but I can't help it. Give them my best respects and kiss little Siss for me.

Your Brother

T.J.Cone

Camp "Ben Hill" Fallen Creek
Andersons division 3rd Brigade
July 26th 1862
My dear friend

Having left home previous to receiving your most interesting letter, it was forwarded to me, and I received it yesterday evening. As soon as I arrived at this place, I was told by Dr. Morgan, a gentleman who stayed at the same house with your Father, that your brother was dead. I couldn't imagine which one of the boys it was. Dr. didn't recollect the name. I was never more astonished in my life.

Your family has sustained a great loss indeed; but you have one consoling thought. That is he died a Christian in a noble cause. I know it is almost an insupportable affliction; but I pray God may Sanctify it for your good. It was a great pity your Father couldn't have got to him before he died; but others happen to worse misfortune. Some come to look for their sons; but not finding them, they die unnoticed, unknown. Oh! what sad desolation has been caused by this unholy war. How many, very many households have been made desolate, by Lincoln's hireling hordes.

I never dreamed that a Confederate soldier would treat one of his comrades, as was Thom. Such men are not fit to live, and deserve the fate of traitors. May God speedily mete out to them their just deserts.

Upon arriving at this place I found our regt. on the south side of James river, 5 or 6 miles from Richmond, near "Drury's Bluff", the point where the Federal gun boats were so successfully repulsed. Our whole division marched from the battlefield across the river to this place. I found that a great many changes had taken place. Genl. Huger has been superceded by Genl. R. H. Anderson. Col. Wright has been promoted to Brigadier General and we are in his brigade. We have in our brigade 5 regiments, 3rd, 44th & 22nd Ga., 44th Ala, and lst La. Capt. Geer of our company has resigned and we will soon have a new captain. But worst of all I found so many of my old friends and acquaintances had fallen by the enemy's bullets. Three from our company were killed instantly; but one professed religion. Four or five of the wounded have died of their wounds. So we have lost 6 or 8 men killed, 8 or 10 wounded. We lost about one hundred and fifty six killed and wounded in our Regt. A great many have since died of their wounds in every company. Our loss was all caused by our officers, that is our General officers, ordering us to charge the enemy's batteries on "Malvern Hill", which any one at a glance might see was impossible. Our loss was terrible in our whole division. Gen. Huger or Genl. M. Gruder were very much censured for ordering the charge. All our loss was caused from whiskey. It is awful to think - --- officers will have to answer for. ---- was sent over here to withstand any attack on Drury's Bluff by land, and also to recruit our strength. All were completely broken down. Out of eleven hundred men we could muster only three or four hundred. The same state of affairs exists in every regt. in our division. We have no Col., no Lt. Col. and no Maj. All our officers are company officers acting as field officers. Ours was once one of the best regts. in service; but since last May it has wonderfully deteriorated. I hope it may soon be able to regain its former popularity.

We are wanting officers only. We have the same men but they want leaders. In a few days more, our number will be less. Those not subject to the conscription bill, will leave us soon. They ought to have been permitted to leave on the 16th; but were not permitted to do so. I hate to part with Pa, perhaps forever; but still I am glad for him to get home once more. I think 16 months is too long, for a man 57 years of age, to be absent from his ----. ---- done his duty faithfully. ---- he has lost two days out of the whole time. He has to undergo too many hardships, and too much exposure to remain here any longer. He has a wonderful constitution; but that ----.

Near Winchester, Virginia
September 29th 1862
My dear friend

Your very kind and interesting letter was received several days since, but situated as I've been it has been impossible for me to answer it as soon as I ought to have done. I don't recollect whether I've written to you since we left Richmond or not; if not, I presume you've ere this heard of our works. We've been on the march now almost two months, and rest assured I've seen "hard, hard times" (not such though as you used *to sing* about). Almost every night we've had to march until twelve oclock, and then lay down, perhaps in the rain, with nothing but the blue canopy of heaven for a covering. Just think of our having been exposed to all sorts of weather, with no shelter whatever, and still so many are the spared monuments of God's mercy. It is true a great many have met their graves; but their names will be remembered as one among those who have given up their life's blood, in defense of their country. Since we left Richmond we've crossed the Potomac three or four times. You can imagine how *pleasant* it was marching at night with wet clothes on, many, many times. I do hope we will not be compelled to cross it again. I'm perfectly willing to remain on this side, for a while at least. There is no telling, though, what may happen, we may cross it again tomorrow.

We are now in camp, three or four miles north of Winchester, how long we will remain here, it is impossible for me to say; but I don't think we will be here for any length of time.

Since I've been on the march, I've seen Jack & John & Mr. Roberts several times. I haven't seen Joe a single time; but hope to soon. Jack, Joe and Milt all seem to be getting along first rate; but like myself, they are getting tired of this unhallowed war. I do hope we will all be permitted to return home in peace once more, soon.

I can't expect to hear from you very often, situated as I am at present; but when we are permanently stationed at anyplace, I shall expect two or three every week. Situated as I am, I shall write to you as often as possible whether I hear from you or not. You needn't expect that to be very often.

At the battle of Sharpsburg (the first fought in Maryland) my knapsack was stolen from me. I was thereby relieved of everything I had, now I have nothing.

As the gentleman by whom I expect to send this to Richmond is about to leave, I must bring this to a close. As I have no postage stamps, and no possible way of getting any, you will have *to pay for this before you can get it*. I am almost ashamed to write to you, and not pay the postage; but I can't help it now. I haven't time to give you a detailed account of the recent battles; but will do so as soon as possible. Give my *very best* respects to the family and all inquiring friends. By the way, I think it is time Samantha was writing to me. I haven't heard from her in a long, long time. I will again as soon as I can. If you write to me again, direct as before.

I remain your true friend.

A.B.S.

Camp near Fredericksburg
31st December 1862
My dear friend

Your very kind and interesting letter of a late date has been rec'd., and I confess I'm unable to describe my feelings, would I were adequate to the task. I had thought that you waited a *very* long time before writing: but from your apology I feel honor bound to excuse you. I ought to have written to you long since; but I've neglected it so long, that I'm heartily ashamed of my conduct. When you for a moment consider the condition in which I was then placed, and the many difficulties under which I labored, I know you will excuse me. Since writing to you last, I've certainly undergone many privations and sufferings. Sometimes I've been without food for an incredible length of time; at others I've been almost destitute of clothing. While at Culpepper I had, what I once thought, the pleasure of seeing a snow storm in all its horrors. Several men in our division were disabled for life. Their feet being frost bit. Since that time we've again been visited by another snow storm and I know it was a beautiful sight; but I must confess I was altogether unfit to appreciate it. Imagine us all crowded around a small fire (for wood was then very scarce), the snow falling thick and fast around us, and you can then form a very incorrect idea of our condition. After all this awful weather came the horrors of the battle field, perhaps the most sanguine of the war. I visited the battle field the day after the battle, and I was so destitute of clothing that I robbed the dead Yankees of such clothing as I needed. I never thought I would be reduced to such extremity; but self preservation is the first law of nature. I know you will think I've become very much degenerated, I confess I have; but under such circumstances I think I might very well be excused. But enough of this dark picture. Let us for a moment turn to the bright side.

Christmas day I had the pleasure of receiving a full suit of clothes from home, besides other things quite as acceptable. I can now bid defiance to the winds and rains. The government, no doubt, has been doing all in its power to make its soldiery comfortable; but still a great many are in a very uncomfortable condition. If we remain in one position any length of time, I think *all* will soon be in a very good condition to stand the winter. We are still without tents. The Government has furnished each company with one tent for the officers. The privates must do the best they can. Some have small tents, captured from the enemy, in which they sleep quite comfortably. It has been said by some that a soldier needed only what he could carry; this is a mistake. A soldier in this climate needs much more than he is able to carry on his person. If one gets *himself* along, *without* any baggage, he does well.

CHAPTER THREE

1863

A busy year in the War – Chancellorsville, the death of Gen. Stonewall Jackson, and of course Gettysburg. In this chapter Alva writes of daily life and other things leading up to the Battle of Chancellorsville and his first hand account of the battle, injuries to old friends, and the heavy loss they suffered. Maragret's brother, Andrew Jackson Cone (18th GA, Co I) also writes from Chancellorsville describing the Battle and of the death of a family friend, Milton Roberts, and being with him as he died. All is not bad though, as Alva reports of having a picnic and party with the "ladies of Virginia". Alva briefly mentions Gettysburg, then professes his love for Margaret, and tries his hand at some poetry.

Camp old U.S. ford Va.
Feb. 15th 1863
My dear friend
Your very kind and interesting letter of a late date, was *recd*. a day or two since, and I needn't tell you, with what feelings of pleasure its contents were perused. In it you remarked that you had *almost* despaired of ever hearing from me again. This time, I *think I will* have written soon enough to dispel all such fears. I confess I've sometimes waited rather long before answering your letters, and I'm afraid that either you have been *guilty* of the same thing, or my letters have been very much delayed in going from this place to *Millwood*. I think *you*

will have to answer immediately, as I've one, or *I will* come to the same conclusion you did in reference to me; that is *despair of ever hearing from you again*. But enough of this foolishness.

You remarked that there was a gentleman in your neighborhood. (Dr. Burke) teaching penmanship. After mature reflection, I must say I haven't the pleasure of an acquaintance with the *honorable* gentleman. If I ever knew him I don't recollect it, I'm inclined to think I never knew him. *As to his being* in the 13th Ga. I can't say; but from my recollection of the forces engaged, I don't *think* that Regt. was in the engagement. I *may* however be mistaken. As to his being a good teacher, I acknowledge; he certainly caused *you* to make great improvement, and had you not told me of your having attended his school, I should have attributed your improvement to your indomitable perseverance, knowing that you possess that quality to such an eminent degree. If, the gentleman, caused such an improvement in all his scholars, *he certainly* (to use a Virginia expression) ought to be allowed to *prevaricate a little*. I expect, before reading this scribbling letter, you will think, a little schooling in penmanship, would not be wholly lost on me. As it is the best I can do, you will have to overlook all deficiences. I hope I shall improve, after having such a preceptor as yourself, that is if the *copies* are *more frequent*. I promise you to do all in my power to profit by the instruction.

You needn't be surprised when I tell you, "*I have the blues*". "I feel like one, who treads alone, some banquet hall deserted". for Miss Mollie *has gone* and married. Alas! for me, do not I deserve pity? Of course, and there being no one here to console me, I am *blue*. But never mind, there is an old proverb that "There are as good fish in the sea as were ever caught out of it"; truly this is encouraging.

You spoke of *your* Christmas as if we poor d-(Oh! I liked to have been guilty of profanity) didn't have any. It is true we didn't have any parties; but we came very near it, as the *Yankees* came very near visiting us without an invitation. I enjoyed myself finely, as I recd. a box from home on Christmas day, concerning which, I think I wrote you in a previous letter.

Since writing to you last I visited Jack, John and Joe, below Fredericksburg, and found them as comfortably situated as any of their "fellows in arms", much better than I am, as they had tents, and

----

Camp near Massaponax Church
Guincy Station, Virginia
April 9th 1863
Friend Mag,

I'm once more in camp, among all my army friends. I arrived yesterday evening, after a most disagreeable travel of four or five days. I found the Brigade at their former encampment, contrary to my expectation as I'd heard that they had moved. Would you think it? I found snow on the ground the 8th inst. There is quite a difference between the climate of this state, and that of our own lovely Georgia. When I left home everything was smiling with the beauties of spring. Here you can see no such enlivening sights. A few trees in the swamps begin to bud, and that is the only sign of vegetation. I've seen very little wheat since I left Richmond. It seems as if the people had given up all notion of raising a crop this year. What little wheat that will be raised in this state, will be needed for home consumption, and consequently the army will have to be supplied by other states, principally Georgia and South Carolina. I hope and believe we will be blessed with an abundant harvest. Truly, our prospects are very flattering indeed.

So soon as I arrived, Capt. Armstrong[1] handed me a letter; from whom, I couldn't imagine. And still more was I perplexed when I opened it, and read- Mr. A.B.Spencer. Dear Sir, So soon however as I read the first two or three lines, I knew whence it came. Now Miss Mag, I *do believe* you felt somewhat vexed when you received my last. I'm sorry, indeed, that I caused you for a moment to suspect that I

---

[1] Captain James Armstrong, CSA

was writing anything "all in jest" as you are pleased to call it. I honestly meant what I said, as I told you when last we met. But enough of this, you *won't believe* but that I'm *flattering* you; although I've repeatedly told you that I never indulged in that, to me a very objectionable practice.

I ought to have written to you long since but there was such a scarcity of news, at home to write about. I thought I would wait until I got to the army, when *possibly* I might obtain some information, that would probably be of some interest to you; but I'm fearful I shall be sadly disappointed. I say "sadly disappointed", for truly it would be a disappointment for me not to write something that would interest my gentle reader. Every thing is in "status quo", as when I left. No change, except that the troops have been ordered to dispense with all unnecessary baggage: which clearly indicates an early active, campaign. This morning the booming of canon could be distinctly heard in the distance. I think it is merely the enemy practicing on the other side of the river. As to an early attack I don't much expect it; although the high winds are drying the roads very fast.

I haven't been to see Jack & the other boys yet; but expect I shall go to-morrow. As all of our band have not yet arrived, I think it very likely I can procure leave of absence. If your Father visits the 18th, I shall be most happy to see him in the 3rd. We will try and give him a little music, I know he is *fond* of that. As for anything else I can't promise, for rations are *beautifully small*. Instead of sugar, we now draw syrup. Occasionally rice, new bacon, and same old quantity of flour- rather the same quantity of *old* flour, I think some of it is quite aged.

The Regt. has just returned from a general inspection, to see condition of arms ammunition etc. What looks something like a fight or some fuss, some time soon doesn't it. But *I* don't expect it much. *My* opinion however is of no service. If our Band had all been present, we should have had a pretty hard time today.

I suppose you are still *President* of "Crozier's Institution". If I should ever go home again on furlough I will be very apt to happen in just in time for you to give recess to your students. I know they will be under everlasting obligations to *me;* for I shall be certain to stay some time, and I heard you say you didn't intend to "take in" until I left. I wish you success.

My respects to every member of the family, "Sis" Mrs. Hall, Eliza, Ann, Babe, Mr. Henry and all my friends and acquaintances.

I hope to hear from you soon.

Your sincere friend
Old A.B.

Camp near Massaponax Church
May 13th 1863
My dear friend

"I'm well at present, and hope these few lines may find you enjoying the same blessing"; after this startling intelligence, I hope you will be prepared to receive whatever of a milder nature that may come afterwards.

It is now the lovely month of May, and the forests and gardens of Virginia, are fast changing their wintry garbs for those of Soul inspiring and health renewing Spring. We had hoped to have enjoyed the first of this lovely month at a picknick party, but our hopes were blasted, as they've often been before. As this reaches you, I expect you will have long since heard the cause of our disappointment. Just for a moment contrast the different ways by which we celebrated that day. While you were enjoying yourselves, perhaps making some nice little *conquest*, your friends were engaged in deadly conflict with the enemy. I can't blame you tho', enjoy yourselves while you can, for *we* can't. It does look a little strange to see a crowd at home engaging in a frolic, while at the same time their absent friends are in midst of battle. Since you can not tell what is going on here you are not culpable. Otherwise you would be. I don't believe as some seem to, that a young lady ought to put on a *long* face at the commencement of war, and never smile during the whole time: "Laugh and grow fat" is my motto. I always look upon the bright side of a picture. Make the best of a bad bargain. It is true it is enough to make any one feel sad to think of the death of so many of our friends, and the total destruction of our once happy and prosperous country; but it may be for the best. You said in your last that you were afraid that you would fail to interest me. You need feel no anxiety on that score; for I assure you they are always interesting and serve to while away many an unhappy hour. I can say in truth, I wish they were longer and more frequent. The only objection I have to any of my correspondents is they don't write often enough. If you had the slightest idea how much pleasure it afforded me to receive letters from those I like, you certainly would exert yourself more. You think that because I'm in the army, I have everything to write about. You are much more greatly blessed in that respect than I am. I, as it were, am completely cut off from the balance of the world; while you have every facility for obtaining knowledge of facts at home and abroad in civil life as in the field. I think I have more need to be fearful than you; but I'm going to try and interest you in *length* of letter, if in nothing else, if I fail it will be gratifying to know that I exerted myself to accomplish the desired object.

On the morning of the 29th, of April, one brigade recd. orders to repair immediately to Gen. Lee's headquarters near Fredericksburg. From thence we went to Gen. Anderson's headquarters near which we encamped. About two oclock we started on the plank road (leading to Orange Courthouse) to meet the enemy who we heard were advancing in force. We went to a hotel on the road called Chancellorsville, but having only three brigades of our Division (about 5000 men), a retrograde movement was determined upon, and we marched back five miles, threw up breastworks, and there awaited reinforcements. McLaws Division arrived during the night. After being in every engagement near Chancellorsville, our brigade was sent to Fredericksburg to meet the enemy who had crossed below the town. Our brigade suffered greatly being inadvance during the whole week's engagement. Our Regt. suffered more than any other in our brigade. The loss in killed & wounded in the brigade amounted to over three hundred; that in our regiment to between one hundred and thirty and one hundred and fifty. One of your acquaintances Jno. Roundtree was shot in the right arm near the elbow. Our surgeon said it would have to be amputated. Jno. objected and the last time I saw him he hadn't done anything for his arm. If it isn't amputated soon, I fear he will lose his life. Maj. Jones (of Covington, Ga.) commanding our regt. lost his arm. Capt. Armstrong of my company recd. a severe wound from shell in his right shoulder which I fear will prove mortal. I would give you a longer and better account of the engagement; but you know I'm no hand for description.

On the 12th of May, we had one picknick. At night we continued the frolic. We arrived in camp about six oclock this morning, not having slept any during the night. You can easily judge my ability to interest you after having gone through such an ordeal. We enjoyed ourselves finely. We had lots of *good victuals*, and plenty of Virginia's pretty girls, the real (F.F.V.s).[2] I had never had such a nice time in my life; but the performances were a little too protracted ("twenty our hours stretch"). I can put up with it tho' as it comes so seldom. There were some very pretty women present; but none as pretty as *Miss* Mollie and others of my acquaintance in Ga. I have enjoyed myself finely since I returned from home. I've been to some half dozen parties and had a splendid time at all of them. While at these parties I almost forget that such a thing as war is in progress; but when I return to camp, to eat nothing but a little piece of meat and about the same quantity of bread, I fully realize the fact.

After the severe engagement on the Rappahannock our brigade returned to its old encampment at this place Saturday morning. The next day I listened in the forenoon to a very good sermon, delivered by Rev. Mr. Potter from Ga., in Massapronax church. In the afternoon Mr. Crumley (from Ga.) delivered a sermon in camp. Prayer meetings have been in progress through the whole brigade

---

[2] First Families of Virginia, a slogan for the socially substanial.

ever since we returned. Several have been baptized. Four from my company have or will join the church. The meetings are still in progress. Our Chaplains are doing all they can I think for the cause of religion.

Since I returned I've made several efforts to procure a pass to visit Jack; but have signally failed every time. Our officers are much more strict on us now than they ever were before. It is almost impossible to get out of camp. It's true I could go without a pass; but I would be certain to be taken up by the "Provost guard" or as some of the boys call them the "Provoking guard". I suppose you (know) I haven't been to Va. yet.

As regards the movements of our army, I think we will remain idle for at least two or three weeks longer, after which time, I think, will commence another active campaign. In the late engagements we gained a signal victory over "fighting Joe" (or as some call him "fainting Joe"); but the Confederacy has sustained a great loss in the death of Gen. Jackson; but I hope more Jacksons will rise up in defense of our cause. Jackson was certainly wounded by our own men.

I hope this very poor letter will interest you some. It will certainly draw your mind from home for a few moments, if nothing else. If you now will write me a long letter I shall be satisfied. My respects to all the family, Mrs. Hall, "Sis" and all my friends especially my scholars. I am much obliged for the information concerning those school accts. & notes. I am yours most respectfully.

A.B.

P,S. I'm glad the Crozier institution is in such a flourishing condition. When you have your examination now just write me, maybe I can come who knows. I have been fortunate so far in getting I *may* be able to come again. A,B.

15th. Joe Graham was here last night. He was just returning from Guincy Station where he had been to look for the Capt's. negro boy who had run away. He couldn't find him, he thinks he has gone to the enemy. Joe looks as well as I ever saw him. He wants to go home very bad. Jack is well. Milt. Roberts poor fellow was killed.

A.B.S.

Fredericksburg, Va.

May 14th '63

Dear Sister,

I received yours a few minutes ago. I was asleep when Bat came, and gave it to me, so if I fail to write you an interesting letter you must look over it.

We have moved back to our old camps, and everything is as quiet as usual out. I don't think that we will stay here long. The camps are mighty dull now, since so many of our boys are gone. Poor Roberts.[3] I saw him fall, and heard him speak his last words. He was as brave a soldier as ever dies. Also was Mike King. Siss, I will try and give you a history of the position we had to charge. It was a very dense forest and the enemy had built works of logs & brush. Also in front of these works, they had cut down trees, fallen in every conceivable manner to impede our progress. So you see we went head long in there and they commenced firing on us.

We halted & put into firing as rapidly as possible. Some lay down others kneeled down, some got behind trees but the trees were so few and little, they did not afford much shelter for the enemy had cut them all down that was of any size. Here we lay under the most murderous fire I ever saw until we got orders to fall back. Which we did in the most disorderly manner, leaving our dead and wounded, those who were too badly hurt to get away themselves behind.

We did not renew the attack, but Jackson coming up in the rear forced them to surrender. What few of the enemy was left recrossed the river. Now the Yanks were in full force between us and Fred----. Then we marched on them forming a line of battle. We started forward just at dusk. The Yankees commenced a retreat at our sight. We pushed on after them with all possible speed. We charged about

---

[3] Milton Roberts, 18th GA., Co. I.

2 miles driving the enemy before us, but could not get close enough to shoot.

We put them across the river that night.

(*Apparently written to Margaret by her brother, Andrew Jackson Cone, 18ᵗʰ Georgia Inf, Co. I*)

Camp Bunker Hill, Va.
July 17th 1863
Dear Friend
Not long since the dull monotony of camp life was again intervened by the reception of another of your most interesting letters. I needn't again tell you what pleasure I experienced in its perusal. Since I last wrote many have been the changes in my company. Our gallant commander Capt. James Armstrong fell at Chancellorsville, besides others of our company. Capt. Sanders[4], promoted since the death of Capt. Armstrong, fell at Gettysburg in Pennsylvania. The loss in our brigade at the latter place was truly alarming. Just think out of 1400 men, 800 should be killed, wounded & prisoners. I am truly thankful that I'm still alive, after having gone through so many hardships, at some future time I will give you an account of our trip, suffice it now to say, I enjoyed myself finely. I saw Jack just before the battle at Gettysburg. I hope he came out safe.

True there is great pleasure in being allowed the privilege of addressing you as a friend and indeed I'm not insensible to the honor; but I would that it were otherwise. Perhaps you will be surprised at the latter clause of the above sentence; but I hope in the course of this letter to give you sufficient reasons for the above seemingly very insulting remark. Should I fail to render the above intelligible, attribute it to mental incapacity, and not to any want of sincerity. You very well know I'm not blessed with any great fluency in the expression of my thoughts; consequently you needn't look for any very elegant or gallant expressions. What I say shall be natural,

---

[4] Captain Dennis N. Sanders, CSA

unaided by any of those artificial adornings so much used. It has been said "Nature when unadorned is adorned the most", and I think truly in some instances; but in the present, I can only say I hope it may prove true.

Having long been acquainted with you and having so often witnessed in you those honorable and prepossessing traits of character which render woman so lovely, I am bold enough (although I'm fearful you'll think it unwarranted) to tell you, that you that something more than a mere sentiment of friendship has unconsciously found its way into my heart. In you I've found perfected, those intellectual, moral and industrious gifts which alone can make one happy. What opinion you've formed of me, I know not; but I'm afraid you've found wanting in me many of those virtues, with which you've so bountifully supplied. In you are concentred all my affections. I know I'm unworthy the respect (much less the love) of one so greatly my superior, as yourself, but why should I keep secret from you the paramount thoughts of my heart, the day star of my existence? What you are to me, words fail to express. I can only say I love *you*, and *you only*. I don't ask you to commit yourself by an affirmative answer. You may never have looked for such a letter as this from me, consequently you may wish time for consideration. I await with pleasure your decision. I only hope for one word of encouragement, and when I see you again I will be courageous enough to tell you in person that which I've just so feebly expressed.

You may think this very unpremeditated; but I assure you, I've long felt ---- for *you* ---- love, I now am bold enough to declare. I ought to have told you this in person long ago. I have no excuse *but fear*. I knew not then as I know not now how to address you on this subject.

"If I speak to thee in Friendships name,
Thou thinks't I speak too coldly,
If I mention Love's devoted flame,
Thou says't I speak too boldly.
Between these two unequal fires,

Why doom me to thus hover?
I'm a friend, if such thy heart requires;
If *more* thou seeks't, a *lover*.
Which shall it be?
Fair one, choose between the two."

Now you understand why I would that you were to me otherwise than a friend. It is not that I esteem you less, but that *I love you more*. I await with anxiety one approving smile, one kind word of encouragement to strengthen my devoted attachment for *you*. Would it be presumptious in me to hope for a favorable return?

Oh! could I but divine the feelings caused by the reception of this letter; it *might* cause me to have less fears and doubts, and to refrain from giving offense to you by expressing sentiments which I know could not be reciprocated. But wisely has Providence kept.

I can't attend the commencement of the C. (I beg pardon) institution; but I will send this letter, my representative, hoping it may be acceptable as he who writes it. I know it will be less embarrassing. Accept my sympathy for the pain caused by the toothache, I fully appreciate it.

My respects to your Father & family, I am very sorry I didn't see him during his last visit to Va.; but under the circumstances I can't blame him. My respects to *Aunt* N., *Sis*, Samantha and *everybody* else of my acquaintance. I shall await with anxiety an answer to this, to you, very unexpected letter. But you say you like to be agreeable surprised. I hope this may be such to you. *Yours sincerely,*

A.B.S.

CHAPTER FOUR

1864

January through June

Alva writes of the monotony of daily camp life, being cold and lonely, and longing for a furlough to come home and see Margaret and his family. In sending Margaret a ring (engagement ring), one he has made himself, it is apparent that he has proposed marriage to her in an earlier missing letter we don't have. Alva speaks of the prospect of reenlisting for two more years. Not something he's fond of, but the "noble thing to do, 'submission is death, or worse than death.'" Military action mentioned in this section is limited to the Wilderness Battle and what is believed to be Spotsylvania, though it is not named as such.

On a picnic at Montpelier, the home of James Madison, he describes the grounds and sites he saw – even picks a souvenir of a cedar sprig from the grave of Madison, to send home to Maggie. Even at that time in history, Montpelier was a historical site. Built by his parents, James and Eleanor Conway Madison in Orange Co., Virginia, Madison grew up there and inherited the mansion after his father's death.

Margaret writes of her great fear of possibly seeing a Yankee while riding a train on a trip that will take her through Andersonville Prison.

Camp "Jennie Hart"
Madison Station, Virginia
January 25th 1864
Dear Mag-

I'm alone now in my little cabin home and as I sit musing over a
cheerful fire, thoughts, happy thoughts of days "now gone forever",
crowd thick and fast to my mind. It is cold and dreary, but the
recollection of the happy "days of yore", warms up, and kindles into
life, those pleasant, happy scenes which have been so long pent up in
my heart and which cannot be forgotten.

To day may gaze, and may forget tomorrow,
But on the hearts pure table, joy and sorrow
Are traced in lines that fade not; we may die
But cannot forget rapture and agony.

The scenes on which my heart most delights to dwell are those
of joy and rapture, not of sorrow and agony. I'm thankful however,
that of the latter I've very few to call to remembrance. The above
may indicate to you that I have the "blues"; but I assure you, I was
never in better "spirits". Don't think now that I've been drinking.
True it is a melancholly thought that we've commenced another year
of suffering and toil, but it is also a pleasant reflection that Kind
Providence assisting us, we've so far been victorious over our ruthless
foe, and that we are now so well prepared to prosecute the war, with,
if necessary, redoubled vigor.

Why is it that the people of Ga. are so desponding? Is it because
of one slight victory obtained over our troops? Let those desponding,
look to the down trodden people of Virginia, for an example worthy
of imitation. The enemy have been in this state ever since the
beginning of our present struggle; they have besieged their capital,
and penetrated almost every nook & corner; but still after all their
trouble and misfortune, they are hopeful, and strongly believe there
is a happy time coming. Not only has the Yankee army been in this

state; but our army, which I'm sorry to say is almost as bad as the Yankee. I'm as strong a defender of Georgia's character, as any one, I really believe she is now, as formerly, the "Empire state of the South"; but I'm sorry to say that I believe the people of Virginia have suffered more with less desponding than the people of Ga. ever could have done. If any, at home, *are* despondent they ought to keep *that* thought hid in their hearts. Let a soldier know that his hardships and suffering are appreciated, and that he has the sympathies of the loved ones at home, he will enter into the prosecution of his duties with more vigor and determination than ever; but on the contrary let him be met (when he goes home) with long faces, and expressions of fear as to our ultimate success, and he will return to his command a worse soldier, and *may* end his life at the stake for desertion. If such be true, what a fearful responsibility must necessarily rest upon those who have so imprudently expressed such opinions. The army of (Genl. Lee) is by no means whipped, why should the people at home be? It is the duty of all to cheer the way worn, disheartened soldier and frown upon desertions and all will be well.

We've corresponded with each other a long, long time and almost invariably I've told you how interesting and how much pleasure your letters afforded me; but still each one waits for the other to answer before writing and by this means a month elapses before we hear from each other. I'll tell you how we can easily avoid it, let us each write once every week. That is, if it be agreeable to *you*. I know it is quite a task; but I believe you'll comply, will you not? You know I'm not due you a letter; but I'd much rather write to you than not, I hope you'll come to the same conclusion. I think I shall continue to write often, unless you otherwise, order it, and they prove uninteresting. I shall write again next week.

You know, that camp life almost invariably renders one reckless, almost every moment he's surrounded by a crowd of noisy, gay companions, whose chief aim is to while away the time as pleasantly as possible; but there are times of some reflection when he is brought to think of those, far, far away at home. One of those pleasant times has now arrived, and there is but one thing ---- ful to render the reverie almost reality. You can conjecture what it is.

I've written this letter in a style calculated to convey the impression that the future looked anything but bright to me. Don't for a moment let such a thought enter your mind; for I assure you I enjoy myself finely, and am determined to "let the wild world wag as it will, I'll be glad and happy still." I wouldn't write in this way to any one else,(for I know what I write to *you*, is for *you alone*). besides if I were despondent, I know it would have no deleterious influence on *you*. I've yet-to learn of the first lady who is despondent, or who is willing to submit to Yankee rule.

The envelope in which this is enclosed is of my own manufacture. What do you think of it. I made two bunches. I like them better than any Confederate ones I can buy. I hope to see you soon. I think I can get a furlough. My respects to the family, Mrs. Hall and *Miss Sis*. Write soon *very* soon.

I remain as ever, yours,

A. B.

Camp "Jennie Hart"
Madison Station Virginia
January 31st 1864
Dear Maggie,

As one week has elapsed since I last wrote, I will again *try* and. interest you, by a perusal of one of my letters, according to promise; for I consider that I have promised; until I find that *you* object to my too frequent requisitions on your time and enjoyment.

I've just been talking with a member of my company who has just returned from home on furlough, and his recital of the many happy scenes through which he there passed, has made me more than ever anxious to visit our own beloved state once more. Not only did he enjoy the "good eating", (of which you know a soldier is peculiarly fond); but from his unusual hilarity, *any one* might *guess*, that he had gained the affections of some fair young lady. "I say *any* one might guess", I didn't have the trouble of guessing, for he told me *all*, of his own accord. I heard you say once, that "we soldiers showed our letters to each other", I then denied it, and deny it still. This looks like a strange contradiction, doesn't it? But I assure you he is my only "confident", consequently he feels no hesitancy in communicating all his secrets to me, and I to him. Months ago I would have been far from making this acknowledgement to you; but as you've, uncalled for, made the same acknowledgement, I deem it due to your own candidness, for me to make the same. Rest assured however, that what you write, will be seen by him and me alone; and if you object (the remotest contingency) myself alone. You know however, that among soldiers "confidants" are "necessary evils". Just think of one's being compelled always to remain silent on that subject which alone absorbs all his thoughts, it is almost equivalent to solitary confinement. Neither of you know each other, what harm can happen? None that I can see.

In all of your letters you seem to be very much reserved, why is it? Is it because you're afraid that I'll prove false or untrue? If that be your excuse banish it at once; for I pledge you my most sacred honor as a gentleman, that I *will* prove true and faithful to the vows I've made. Your sweet "image is engraven on my heart" and I could not, desired I ever so much, erase it. True we've never *talked* to each other of love; but we've *written*, and I consider that a ready evidence of our mutual affection. *I* have always unreservedly told you all, kept back nothing. Had I the slightest intention to deceive, I shudder at the word, I could never have been so heartless as to express myself in so open a manner. I can't believe you think I would deceive. I'm already heartily ashamed of what I've just written.

Please pass it over, and take no offence; for I assure you, if I were to offend, or cause you even one moment to doubt, I should be very, very unhappy. I will never again allude to such, even should you accuse me.

Furloughs still continue to be granted with more than usual liberality, and with it, my prospect, of seeing you once again this winter, is brightening. We've already made one very necessary step, the gaining of our Brig. Gens. consent. He has kindly told us that, "he thought there would be no difficulty about our getting a furlough the last of Feb. and that he would exert all his influence to obtain it for us". Thus far we feel very much encouraged. The prospect of so soon seeing Father, Mother, Sister and *You*, makes the time pass off much more swiftly and pleasantly, I assure you; for I *had* looked for a dull, dreary, unpleasant winter. If we fail, we can, at least, enjoy the anticipation. I hope I shall soon surprise you as before; and then I will tell you in words, that which I've so often tried to write. I know I shall have but, twenty four days, to go and come; but if it takes all to visit you, I'm resolved to take it I expect to stay only a day or two at home, and then I shall start for Millwood.

I know I love Father, Mother and Sister as affectionately as ever son or brother could; but the love I have for you is of a far different kind; consequently I will make *any* sacrifices, to obtain that one desire of my heart, to see you. If I don't come in March, you needn't expect me until next year. It does look like a long, long time; but no desires of mine can alter it, so I can but wait, wait, wait.

The quiet of our encampment has been somewhat disturbed for the last day or two, by reports that the enemy was moving his forces, seemingly, preparatory to an advance; but I believe the excitement has all subsided and we again once more at rest. The unusual long *spell* of pleasant weather recently, caused the enemy to collect his army at Culpepper "C.H."[1] for review, and I suppose that was the cause of all our uneasiness. I do sincerely hope that the weather may grow worse and worse until we get our furloughs; for with pleasant weather *all* our hopes are blasted. We know too well what the spring campaign will be. Still we doubt not our success.

So far, no proposition, has been made to our Brigade, for reenlistment; but I've no doubt that when it is made, all will

[1] Culpepper Court House

magnanimously respond to it. The prospect of the war lasting two years longer is truly a sad thought; but we all know that Submission is death, worse than death; con-sequently we are all resolved, if fall we must, to fall nobly when duty calls us. A great many of our brigades have reenlisted, doing honor to themselves and cause.

Excuse the many mistakes I've made in this uninteresting letter, I will do better in my next. If I've said anything amiss, I pledge you my word it is altogether unintentional. Write to me every week, and thereby grant the greatest blessing I could desire. Will you?

My best respects to your Father's family, Mrs. Hall, *Miss Sis*, and believe me Dearest one.

Yours devotedly,

A. B.

"Camp Jennie Hart"
Feb. llth 1864
Dear Maggie
I delayed writing to you on last Sunday contrary to my previous determination, on account of circumstances wholly beyond my control. The enemy crossed the Rapid Ann at Moreton's ford, on our extreme right, and at Barnett's ford on our extreme left, at both of which places there was a short but spirited engagement; our brigade, for a wonder, was not engaged. About twelve oclock Saturday night, we received orders to be ready to march at daylight. Accordingly at the first appearance of dawn, we started off in the rain to go *somewhere*, we knew not where. After marching nearly all day we arrived in camp, completely broken down. I was never in my life so tired. I could hardly sleep for pain. we are now once more quietly ensconced in our *cosy little shanty*, and *hope* to remain so, for some time yet to come. I think it was the intention of the enemy to make a raid on Gordonsville; but I'm happy to say they were handsomely foiled at every point.

Yesterday evening I received another of your most welcome letters, and I needn't again tell you how happy it rendered me. I will only say, I've read it over three or four times since its reception, and each time its perusal seems to carry me nearer and nearer to *you*. I'm very glad indeed that Jack has such a fair prospect of getting home, and that too for so long a time; for as you say, I think those who have been in service almost ever since the war began are more entitled to enjoy the pleasures of home than those who have so far done nothing for their country. I hope he will succeed; but when one once gets into service, it is hard, very hard for him to get out. When a person, however is appointed to a civil office, it is much easier.

I'm very glad your school is in such a prosperous condition. You say "your time is so much engaged that I mustn't expect long. letters", I'm really sorry for that but I'll tell you a way by which you can easily remedy *that*, write once a week as I do. *That* will remedy it to some extent; but you know how much more pleasant it would be to receive a *long* letter, no matter how long; but of course it is discretionary with yourself, still I *desire* long and frequent letters. I hate however to make such frequent draughts upon your time; but I believe you will grant this simple request.

Since we've been encamped in our present winter quarters, I've amused myself to some extent by making rings of bones, *beef bones*. I will bring you one, provided I get a furlough; if not, probably I will send it by mail if you wish. It is not equal to a gold one; but *I* think "it does right well" considering.

We expect our furloughs next Monday or Tuesday approved or disapproved, we hope & believe the former. If I do come home, I shall visit *you* provided all my time is not taken up there, as has been the case with several of my Regiment recently. No connections are made on the different roads between here and home, except occasionally,

Camp "Jennie Hart" Virginia
23rd February 1864
Dear Maggie,

I've delayed writing to you for sometime, hoping that very soon I should have the exquisite pleasure of answering your last in *"propria personae"*; but it now seems that I'm doomed to disappointment again. Our furloughs have been gone, now, six or seven days, and it does seem as if they were gone for good. They will certainly be in this evening or not at all.

A day or two since I received a letter from Father informing me that Mother had received a severe fall, and he was afraid that it might prove serious. I haven't received any additional information, since his first announcement. This information makes me more than ever anxious to receive our furloughs. I know however that if there is sickness in our family, it will greatly interfere with my expected visit to Dooly; if that is the only difficulty, however, I shall try and come anyhow. I never yet attempted anything, which promised me much pleasure, but something was sure to happen to prevent. I am almost ready to exclaim "Oh! ever thus from childhood' hour I've seen my fondest hopes decay etc. etc." I'm almost afraid to start home, for fear I will cause you to be disappointed, and I assure you I want to see you almost, if not quite as bad, as my relations. I know too, exactly what you'll think no matter what excuse; but I believe you would give all excuses due consideration before coming to any determination. I'm not certain yet whether not I shall be so fortunate as to receive a furlough; but if I do receive one rest assured I shall use every effort in my power to see you; if I fail I shall lay the case before you, and you an acquit or sentence me just as you see proper. In giving you the power acquit or condemn however, I reserve to myself the right to say which decision I prefer. You know which I prefer, so if the evidence is not sufficient to admit of an acquital, *you must bribe the* Judge *and Jurors*.

Sunday evening Genl. Wright's lady, two daughters and Mrs. McWhorter arrived in camp. Just the *sight* of a woman, makes us feel a little less like outcasts. There are now some ten or twelve ladies near our camp, wives of different men in our regt. The sight of so many soldiers, I suppose, is quite interesting and novel. It is all quite romantic in camp; but any thing but that, on the march. I suppose they will *all* leave before active operations commence.

Nothing of interest has transpired since I last wrote, save the reenlistment of our Brigade for the war. The 3rd Ga. taking the lead, the rest following. Almost the entire corps of Genl. A. P. Hill's[2] have reenlisted. Those who didn't reenlist, have, by a recent act of Congress, been conscripted.

My respects to Miss *Sis*. The mail is about to leave so I must close. Love to all. Hoping to see or hear from you soon I remain as ever yours devotedly,

A.B.

Camp "Jennie Hart"
Madison Station Virginia
29th Feby 1864
Dear Mag,

I have postponed writing to you longer than I should have done, had I not expected in this to have seen you. As my fate however is so far as I can judge sealed for this winter, I will begin at once. I shall try and interest you by a faint description of the manner in which we pass away this dull monotonous life. You, I suppose, are aware that there are certain duties incident to camp life, which are required to be performed daily. These duties fail, to a great extent, to comsume the whole time, consequently there are enough idle hours for air castle building and retrospection. With all the arduous duties imposed, there are moments when sweet memory wafts us back to the beautiful "long ago". The reflections are mingled with pleasure and pain. Mine, for the past week or two, has been the most happy; for I've been living in anticipation of the happy time I should soon have in

---

[2] Lieutenant General Ambrose Powell Hill, CSA

seeing you and telling you how much I love you. True I've had some enjoyment in thinking of by gone scenes; but by far the greatest has been the prospect of so soon being in your presence. In thinking of the past, my mind would naturally turn to my school-boy days, now "almost forgot". Ah! how plainly do I see the old school house, its enchanting groves, its beautiful flowers, so full of hallowed associations. All seeming to welcome me again. How vividly are those familiar faces pictured to my imagination. The face of some fair-haired, sunny eyed girl, object of my *first* boyish *love*, or of some gay romping boy, meet me at every turn reminding me of scenes which had long since been treasured up as the brightest jewels of my heart. I in my imagination pass along those once beautiful walks or wind my way through those enchanting groves the "living witnesses" of so many of my boyish sports.

"Up springs at every step, to claim a tear, Love little Friendship, formed and cherished here, And not the lightest leaf, but trembling turns With golden visions, and romantic dreams!"

But ah! when I look again through that large crowd of youthful playmates for some dear familiar face, I know too well that he is numbered among the dead. Alas how often do I see in some newspaper an account of the death of some loved one whom I've not seen since last at school. It makes my heart grow sad when I think of those dear ones lying upon some "hard fought little field" unwept save by his weeping Father or his heart broken Mother.

Well do I remember the *Chapel* with its honored professors, its numberless students, and the *old bell* which has so often awakened me from my peaceful slumbers at early dawn, summoning me to the chapel, thus to answer to my name. Ther to listen to those fervent prayers so often made to God in our behalf.

Never shall I forget the last day of our college course, when our entire class came out upon the stage to listen to the farewell address of one of our dear comrades. 'Twas then I felt as if I was parting from all that was dear to me on earth, and my heart was only partially relieved by a flood of tears. Where are those loved ones now? Ah!

"echo answers where". Some "I've not seen for years", others have perished upon the battlefield, others by the hand of disease.

Well do I remember when first I launched my little barque upon the dangerous sea of life. Amidst a Father's affectionate words of encouragement and a Mother's tender "God bless you", I left my quiet home to earn a livelihood, by teaching. I remember too how easily I overcame those difficulties, which at first seemed to me so entirely beyond my mastery. I was surrounded by a crowd of interesting scholars nearly all of whom have been forgotten. But the face of little Emma I can *never* forget.

She was a beautiful girl, a promising obedient scholar, and I could but love her. But soon that beautiful flower was doomed to fade away and die. She was taken sick suffering greatly. So soon as I found that her condition was a critical one I went to see her, and as I sat by her bedside, watching as it were the passage of her spirit from earth to Heaven, she faintly murmured my name, and whispered "Good bye". 'Twas then my heart was inconsolable. Little girl, though she was, I can never forget her, and her last dying words "Good bye" have a charm for me which all time will fail to destroy.

I remember too the first day I arrived at your Father's house in my *two wheeled buggy* Your Father being absent I believe it was you who so kindly interested me until his return. Having accomplished everything I desired, I left the next day with a light heart, full of glorious anticipations. And then the thought of living in such a family was truly encouraging, and I was indeed happy.

Everything pleased me. The scholars were obedient and intelligent and I could but be delighted in instructing them. All went along as smoothly as I could wish. But when the tocsin[3] of war sounded through our land, I determined to be among the first to respond to my country's call. But when I thought of breaking the attachments which I had so recently formed, I was truly sad. I own *now*, that when I parted from "you all" that it required my strongest efforts to suppress my emotions, which if indulged, would have been

---

[3] A signal, or alarm.

at that time and place, wrongly construed by those who might chance to be witnesses. I could not have felt worse, had I been leaving my own Father, Mother and Sister, for your Father's family had been all those to me. How could help feeling regret at parting? Otherwise it would have been unnatural.

And always when I returned from my daily labors to be met by your approving smiles was surely encouraging, and had I known *then*, that which I know *now*, I would indeed have been happy, very happy.

But alas! when I in my imagination again sit around that family board, I see one seat vacant, and I am again reminded that Death too has visited that family, and ruthlessly torn away one of its brightest members. Thom was truly a brave and chivalrous youth. For him I formed a lasting attachment. In his death, our country has lost one of its most efficient and promising soldiers, your family one of its brightest ornaments. It is a consolation, to us all however, to know that he was a professor of religion and that he is now a soldier of that army of redeemed spirits above, where "Sickness and sorrow, Pain and Death are feared and felt no more."

And when I turn my mind forward, I see pictured before me the most beautiful country the "sun ever shone on." Peace and Prosperity smiling upon us, and the proud nations of the earth honoring and admiring us. Oh 'tis indeed gratifying to me to believe such will be our fate.

And then to think, that when we return home laden with honor and crowned in victory, that we shall receive the smiles and approbation of a free people is "joy unspeakable." That such will speedily come I haven't the slightest doubt. I already beg to see a little of the "silver lining" of the dark and lowering clouds which have so long hung over our afflicted country. That the noble action of our armies has caused this, I'm confident. Just think of the way worn veterans of an hundred battle fields, nobly stepping forth reenlisting for he knows not, cares not how long. Does that look like submission? Doesn't it argue success? We already begin to see its effect. We have to-day a better, more efficient army than ever before.

We are better fed we are better clothed so if God is with us, all the hordes of Lincolndom will fail to subjugate us and we will soon be a free & prosperous people.

March 6th 1864. You will see by the date of this, that it has been sometime since I commenced it. I would have mailed it before, had I not been called off on a march. I expect by this time you've received all the particulars relative to the late raid on the Central railroad and Richmond. I know only the part, enacted by our brigade. We were carried in the *cars*, to Frederick Hall, a station on the Central rail road about thirty two miles below this place, where we remained several days. We had a pretty hard time, the weather being extremely cold and disagreeable. On this trip I received your last and situated as I was there, I assure you it was more than ever welcome. I'm perfectly satisfied with the disposition you made of my request to write once every week. I couldn't reasonably expect letters oftener than you have decided. I assure you, however, that if they came every day I would never become wearied. To wait a month before hearing from you is truly disheartening.

You say "we've never talked to each other *personally* about *love*". True we have not. I assure you, had I thought I could have seen you soon, I never would have written a word about it; but gone to you and *told* you *all*. You know that I cannot go home when I wish. Since I last wrote our furloughs have been returned, disapproved, and in all probability it will be twelve months or more before I can see you. Am I then to be kept in such awful suspence, and for so long a time? I do not believe Mag, you would doom me to such unhappiness, such sad disappointment. I know, Mag, from the tenor of your letter, that you wish to ask me something. Am I not right? Is there not some point about which you are dissatisfied? Ask it and if it be in my power I will surely answer it. I desire very much that you should ask it; for I wish to dispel everything that is antagonistic to our love.

Every time I have written to you, I have told you *all*, not one thought has been omitted. Could I remove every doubt, every fear, so that you would write to *me* in the same way, I would be the happiest of men. Tell me those doubts, those fears and I will remove them. Did I say "those doubts"? I retract; for you have just told me "you had more confidence in me than doubt my *many vows*", and I believe you. I know however, that there *is* something about which you are not satisfied. Let me entreat you to give me an opportunity of relieving your mind. I think it is due you and due me to know all. Will you ask me? Will you tell me all?

My letter is so long, I'm afraid you will get tired of reading it so I will stop. I hope in your next you will gratify all the requests I have made in this. My respects to all of the family & Miss Sis.

Your Sincere admirer,

A. B.

Millwood, Ga.

March 2nd 1864

Dear Mr. Spencer,

Yours of 11th ult. was rec'd., little more than a week since & contents read with much pleasure.

I would have answered it previous to now, but I've been expecting or rather hoping to see you, and if not that, at least to receive a letter, in which, this far have been disappointed.

I wish I knew whether your furlough was approved or not. Then I would know better how to write, though I've almost decided that you are not coming, otherwise, you would have been here before now, that is if you rec'd. your furlough at the time expected. I shall be disappointed if you do not come. You have so far been greatly blessed and I hope will continue to be.

A personal discussion of the subject which we have for some time been writing about, would, you must know, be more satisfactory and relieve my mind considerably, not that I attach any want of sincerity to what you have written, for I placed the utmost confidence in you, otherwise, I could never have made the acknowledgement I have.

Pa is going to Vienna[4] tomorrow, I hope to get a letter from you. In my last I told you I could not conveniently write you more than once in two weeks. So soon, however, as my school is up, I will write more frequently. I expect my last was quite old when you rec'd. it, as I've since learned it lay in the office several days before ------

(Incomplete letter from Margaret L. Cone to Alva B. Spencer)

Millwood, Ga.
March 11, 1864
Dear Alva,
Having despaired of seeing you soon, I will no longer delay writing. If you are disappointed in your expectations, I shall be very sorry. You will not be the only one *sadly* disappointed I assure you. I would like much to see you.

This morning I attended the burial of Parson Aldridge. He died the 9th after a linger illness of three weeks. His demise is much lamented by this vicinity. He was buried with Masonic honors, over at the church. I think there were nearly three hundred people present. Within the last month, death has visited many families in this neighborhood.

Dr. Cross has been very sick for a length of time, and now, as he is recovering, the news has come that his son Andrew (who has been a prisoner for eight months in Ohio) is dead. It really seems that he cannot survive this affliction. You doubtless recollect him, he was quite a possessing young man when he left; but death is no respecter of persons. Therefore how important it is for us all to prepare for it, while we are in the enjoyment of good health and surrounded with many, many blessings, how apt ---- are we to forget the God that bless assured how unthankful we are. Consequently sickness & death, are sent upon us to remind us that this earthly home is not our abiding place, but that we should "seek a place in heaven".

---

[4] Vienna, Georgia

I rec'd. a letter from you last week. The contents were perused with much pleasure. I'm sorry of your Mother's misfortune, hope she will recover.

Were you to visit your home & not visit us, 'I should believe your excuse justifiable before hearing it, for I know nothing but such a one would forgive you.

Jack was at Greeneville, Tenn. when we last heard, we are rather hoping to see him home soon.

His division are going to be mounted soon, & there will be some detailed to come home after horses, we hope he will be one of the number. Pa has sent his commission to him, of the opportunity, I wrote you, we haven't heard from him since. I don't know how he will come out.

Capt. Collins has ---- that army as a ---- , though he thinks of not staging such a thing after they are mounted, as it will be difficult for him to remain with them.

It is thought by some, Longstreet intends making a raid in Ky. I hope Jack will get home before that is done. In this there shall be a great effort made ---- as can to bring this war to a close & I am of the opinion that the principal part of the fighting will be done in Virginia. The enemy ---- they are ready to leave it. The "-----" as you call it, is becoming a place of much note. We are going to have preaching this month by the "Hard Shells". Meeting next Sabbath. All send love. I hope to get a letter from you tomorrow.

Please do not show this scrib----

(Incomplete letter from Margaret L. Cone to Alva B. Spencer)

Camp near Madison Station Virginia
14th March 1864
Dear Mag

Yesterday I was made the happy recipient of your last most interesting and welcome letter. I hardly know whether to answer immediately or not, since you have decided for us to write but *once* during two weeks. So anxious, however, am I to tell you what were my emotions Upon its reception, I cannot resist the temptation.

Do you know, Mag, that your letters are my chief delight? Oh, you know not with what rapture, I break the seal and read over and over again your dear letters. I see nothing, I hear nothing, but *you* in every word, in every letter. It seems to transport me to your side, and with rapturous imagination, I gaze into your lovelit eyes and tremble with delight at the varied fascinations of your sweet countenance. And when I sit down to answer them, each scratch of the pen seems to draw us nearer and nearer together, 'til space is annihilated, and our spirits at least, mingle in delightful converse. Do you wonder at my so frequent requests to write often? Indeed, could you conceive how much pleasure they afford me, you would not consider me too *presumptions* in my frequent demands, or requests rather. Every day I go to our Post Master to see if there is any letter for me. Although I know if there is one, he will give it me; still I go, for by so doing, I save a few moments of expectation. When any of my mess mates get letters and I fail, I almost think vengeance upon *all* connected with the Post Office department. I never complain of you for I know the delay is not caused from any neglect on your part. Indeed, your frequent letters have made pleasant many of my lonely camp hours. You have written to me oftener than I could reasonably have expected. How can I ever repay you? I can return you my sincerest thanks. If my letters afford you any pleasure, surely their frequent visits, have, to some extent, compensated you; but I am sure I never can write anywhich will give *you* as much pleasure as your last did me. I had hardly recovered from my recent marches in search (of) Yankee raiders, and I confess I was a little "blue".

Although it was not as explicit as I could wish, still I was very happy and thank you very much.

You still say "a personal discussion of love would be more *satisfactory*, and would *relieve* your mind *considerably*". I know it would Mag, and I myself would much prefer it; but how am I to do otherwise than write. True, as I said in a previous letter, I could wait; but I can't believe you would doom me to such sad disappointment, such agonizing suspense. In my last I requested you to tell me the cause of your dissatisfaction. It is indeed, a source of great anxiety and uneasiness, to know that you are only partially satisfied, and I earnestly request you to tell me all. I will do anything to satisfy you. I assure you it is gratifying to me to know that my efforts to prove my sincerity have not been in vain. In doing that, however, I am confident I have omitted something which causes you uneasiness. I can't imagine what it is, it seems as if I had said everything. It is not too late yet to rectify the mistake; if I but knew what it was. Perhaps in my eagerness to tell you all, I have offended; if so forgive me, It was not intentional I assure you. If we could see each other I know we would be better satisfied; but that being impossible how can I do otherwise than ask you to tell me by letter? Surely you wouldn't condemn me to such suspense, when you can so easily avoid it! Your sympathizing disposition tells me "No". My trusting heart tells me "No". I believe you will not, and am happy; you know not how happy.

You say you know who sent you that Valentine, I wish I knew, for I'm beginning to get jealous. You must tell me who he is, the next time you write. I assure you I didn't write any; but I saw a good many *written*, and I wouldn't be surprised if the one you received wasn't one of them. I didn't receive any. You must tell me all about Miss Samantha's ; for she has a joke on me about the one I received while at your house and I want to get even with her.

I have no news to write, that will interest you; for I know you receive the daily journals, all the important information connected with the army, as soon, almost, as we do. I will only mention the fact, that yesterday evening an order came to our Brigade, stopping all furloughs, until further orders. What gave rise to this order; I'm unable to say positively; but "Madam Rumor" says it is to clear the railroads in order to transport Genl. Longstreet's[5] Corps to General Johnston[6]. Genl. Longstreet and staff were at Orange C.H. a day or two since. I should like very much, for Genl. Longstreet's command to join Genl. Lee again. I have many friends there. I should like very much to see. I believe however there is greater need of them in the west; for I think there is little apprehension to be felt for this army. If Genl. Longstreet does come here, I shall at once begin to mend my *harness*, for a trip into Pennsylvania or Ohio.

I'm sorry to disappoint you by not coming to see you this winter; but I assure you I don't believe it is half as great a disappointment to you as to me. Since the disapproval of my furlough, I can but now look forward to next winter, with more than ever, happy anticipation. It will indeed render the hardships of summer less wearisome; for I will always be buoyed up with the happy thought that then I will *surely* be successful.

There is only one thought that makes the approaching campaign, appear gloomy, and that is the thought that I will almost entirely be debarred the privilege of hearing from you. Perhaps we may go into Pennsylvania or some other *foreign* land, and then I know I will not only fail to receive *your* letters; but be unable to send my own. I will make up for lost time, tho, when I get back into *civilization*.

I thank you very much for your promise to write oftener when your school is out. I only *wish* it was out now.

We are anticipating some *fun* in camp soon. I will write you all about it the next time I write, provided we have it. My respects to your Father's family, Mrs. Hall and Miss Graham. I look for a letter this evening. I will write again soon. *Write again* soon.

I remain as ever yours most devotedly.

A.B.

---

[5] Lieutenant General James Longstreet, CSA

[6] Believed to be Brigider General Joseph Eggleston Johnston, CSA

Madison Station Virginia
March 22nd 1864
Dearest Mag,

Your last, most interesting letter was received this evening, and I thank you very much for so signally making me happy; for I am more happy than ever before. Do you know why your last caused me so much more pleasure than your previous ones? It was the manner in which you commenced it. *You*, no doubt, thought that you were expressing yourself too freely, *I* do not though. Those *two words* tell me of far deeper affection, than anything you have ever said since I first offered you my heart and hand. I never, until now, knew what joy there was in being thus addressed by one whom I so dearly love. Mag, I don't believe you have any idea how much I do love you. But when I think of how much I love you, and that you should then be dissatisfied, it makes me sad indeed. If your dissatisfaction is caused merely from not receiving my addresses and declarations in person, let me entreat you to forego that pleasure, which you now know is absolutely beyond your own or my control. I know I am wholly unable to express all I feel, in a letter. I have tried in every letter to tell you; but I must acknowledge I've not been satisfied with a single one I have written. Every thought seems to have been poorly worded, and failed to express my true feelings. I would give *anything* if I could be with you now, if, for the time, only, I shall consume in writing this letter. I would tell you a great deal more, and that too with far more satisfaction, to *you*, and to me. I have used every effort in my power to see you; but have so far been sadly unfortunate. I still hope on, hope ever. I know the longer my visit is delayed, the more happy I shall be to meet you. My not receiving a furlough has caused more than you or I to be disappointed. I think, the next time I intend applying, I won't say anything about it to any one, and then no one will be disappointed, and if successful I will surprise *all* agreeably or disagreeably, I can't say which.

It pains me very much to hear of the recent deaths in your neighborhood. Oh would that I could of something more consoling, to the bereaved, than my sympathy. I knew both Mr. Aldridge and Andrew, and in them found an exemplary, useful Christian and a promising, upright youth. May God bless and protect the afflicted widow, and the bereaved parents.

If I were at all competent to give you and interesting account of the manner in which I've spent the past week, I would gladly commence at once; but for fear I will not interest you, I shall give merely a synopsis. Last Tuesday Genl. Wright and staff, had what they called a Tournament. It was this, some ten or twelve men were to contend for certain prizes, and those most successful were to crown the most beautiful lady in the assemblage, "Queen of love and beauty". Two posts were placed in the ground about fifty yards apart, one having the representation of a person's head, from the other was suspended a small ring. The knights, for such were these men styled, were, by riding at full speed past these posts, to cut off the head and take the ring with their sword. Each knight was to ride five times. After all had ridden their appointed number of times, they all drew up in line in front of the audience. The first prize was awarded to Capt. Milledge, of the "Milledge Artillery" of Georgia, the second to J. H. McWhorter of the 3rd Ga., the third to C. H. Howard of the 48th Ga., and the fourth to Lieut. J. K. Evans Adjutant General of our brigade. The successful knights were all Georgians. After the prizes were awarded each knight crowned his lady. I knew only two of the ladies crowned, Mis Carter a refugee from Vicksburg and Miss Sallie daughter of Genl. Wright. All went off very pleasantly and I enjoyed myself finely. There was quite a crowd present to witness the performance. Lieut. Genl. Hill, Maj. Genl. Heth and Brig. Genl. Kirkland were among the number.

On Thursday night I attended a ball, given to the knights of the tournament, by Genl. Wright's family, and had the pleasure of seeing many *pretty young ladies*; but I must say there was no comparison to our Georgia ladies. I don' say this because I am a Georgian, but because I honestly believe it. Dancing was kept up until twelve when we partook of a *splendid* supper, which I of course, enjoyed very much. After supper we returned to the ball room, and continued until "*broad daylight*". Before closing this description I will try and give you some idea of the *hall*. It consisted of a large framework of pine *poles*, covered with tent "flys". A floor was laid, and it answered admirably. The inside of the hall was beautifully adorned with wreaths of cedar extending 'round the entire room. In the centre hung two *exquisite* chandeliers trimmed with the same never fading green. All seemed to enjoy themselves finely. I've no doubt you will think I did wrong in attending this ball, until I tell you I was *ordered* there by Gen. Wright. I can't say as some do, that dancing is in itself wrong; but harm may be mad of it, as can be done of almost every amusement; but I don't mean to argue this point. I refrain from it, partly because I can not dance; but mainly because my church has decided it to be wrong, and I am willing to abide by every rule they in their wisdom have established.

A day or two since I was very much amused at a little incident that happened in my company. Sergeant ---- received a nice little silk tobacco pouch, by mail, from a young lady he had never heard of, nor had ever seen. He was the perfect picture of surprise, and I could but laugh when he asked me if I knew the lady; for I was as ignorant as he. He, however, after considering my advice, wrote a short note acknowledging its reception, and soliciting a correspondence. Although a tobacco pouch may seem an an insignificant present; yet when they are received with a little card I bearing the name of some fair lady, they are most dearly cherished, and never fail to awaken the liveliest emotions. Almost every soldier returning from home, has some such remembrances dangling from his coat button. If we ask him who gave it to him, he will tell a long, but to us interesting, story of some fair one at home. Such little souvenirs are always thankfully received, and never fail to cheer the *way worn* soldier, and he knows too that he is not entirely forgotten by those who are so far away. I send you a *very poor ring*, please accept it with *all* my love. It is the best I can do now. I intend sending you a nice one soon if I can possibly get the material. Please direct your letters hereafter as I have written it on the first page, I'm afraid some of your letters will be lost. Write soon. You know not how I long to see you. Love to all. Miss Sis & Mrs. H. I remain as ever your most devotedly,

Alva

Co. "C" 3rd Ga. Regt. Wrights' Brigade,

Army of Northern Virginia

Camp Madison Station Virginia

April 4th 1864

Dearest Maggie,

I must confess that the contents of your last, a little surprised me. In the first place, I will say that I haven't written to Mr. Holtzclaw since I told you of my love. I am certain I never wrote him anything concerning you previous to our engagement; consequently I *know* he knows nothing of the feelings existing between us. I have known him for many years, and found him to be an honorable gentleman. I know him to be one of my strongest friends, and I don't believe he would do anything to injure me. He guessed our true situation, and told it to Billy, in order to find out *exactly* whether his surmises were true or not. I confess I must blame him a little for using such means to gain the desired information; but I'm confident he bore me no malice. I would write to him immediately and seek an explanation if I were not certain it would then reveal that he so much desires to know. I think the best plan I can do is to use a camp phrase, "*let it rip*". Let me assure you that I make our engagement no public story. But *one* person has ever read your letters. I have read portions of them to a few of my most intimate friends; but they didn't even know your name or where you lived.

I have no interesting camp news to record; for it has been exceedingly dull here for a week or more past, and I must say that the long delay of your last was more the cause of my unusual gloominess than any thing which transpired here. The weather for the past week has been extremely bad and disagreeable, causing us to remain in our houses the greater part of the time; consequently there remained nothing for us to do, but to think, think of the loved ones far away. Day before yesterday morning, I arose from my *"feather* bed all *bustin* with straw"* to again see every thing covered with, to us, the beautiful white of snow. Had the ground been dry, I think it would have accumulated to a much greater depth than that of a few weeks previous of which I wrote you in my last; but soon the rains came and it all melted away like beautiful frost work before a summer's sun. It continued to rain throughout the entire day, and soon the *romantic* little *branch*, upon the banks of which our winter cabin is erected, became a mighty, rolling riv --- ulet, I had almost said *river*. Yesterday the sun shone out occasionally; but the broken clouds were flying across the heavens in almost every direction, and the wind blowing a perfect gale; thereby preventing the appearance of our *lady soldiers* at the *chapel*. We have preaching almost every night, and there seems to be great interest manifested by the troops. Our chaplain is of the Methodist denomination, and I must say he is not altogether as interesting as a great many others to whom I have listened; but I presume he does the *best he can*.

If any change has taken place, most assuredly, it has been of a strengthening and not of a weakening character. We can not prove faithless to those we love. So far from it, that we consider ourselves the more happy, when we are permitted to love and be loved in return. This indeed is the true meaning of our happiness. The preference of the ladies for those at home, luxuriating in ease and plenty, to those in the field enduring hardships and deprived *sometimes* of the necessaries, *always* the luxuries of life, is, undoubtedly, their privilege; but I must say *they* are the faithless, not we. I speak only of those guilty of the above charges. Not one word or letter is intended for you. I know a good many, however, to whom it is personally applicable. If I should be so fortunate as to ever get home, I will tell them of it too. I know some young men who have been treated in a manner very unbecoming ladies. Why such has been the case I can't tell to save my life. There was no cause, for such treatment, that I could see.

If such a state of affairs continues, I am afraid I will be compelled to join in with John Graham in reference to the fair sex. They ought to be very careful how they wound the feelings of those in the field battling for *their* liberties. All they desire is the approving smiles of those at home and they will speedily conquer an honorable, lasting peace. I do hope they will not withhold it from us now in our last efforts.

As I anticipated, it is again raining, and I do feel so thankful; for the old proverb "more rain more rest" is certainly true in our situation. So long as it continues bad weather we are sure to remain in our present quarters. I know it will not be long before we will have to commence anew our marches; but I want to postpone the evil day as long as possible. I know if I once get out of these pleasant quarters, it will, in all probability, be several months before I'm permitted to rest again. We all look forward to the approaching campaign with great interest; for we are confident that if successful, twelve months from to day, we can see a termination of hostilities between the North and South. *All* are confident of success, and await only the approach of Grant[7] to show their renewed determination to be free. Don't despond; but have a brave heart, and encourage the soldiers all you can, and I believe you will soon see a free and happy people.

I am truly glad to know that the "Crozier institution" is in such a prosperous condition, I wish the fair instructress *much* success. Being under your gentle influence, your interesting instructions, and seeing every day unmistakeable evidences of your noble and amiable disposition, how could your scholars help loving you? I do not wonder at it at all. I know that *I* couldn't withstand your charming qualities, and the more know of you, the more I see to admire and love.

---

[7] Lieutenant General Ulysses Simpson Grant

Millwood, Georgia
April 10th 1864
Dear Alva,

Since I last wrote, I've had the pleasure of reading two more most interesting and welcome letters from you, and have taken the earliest opportunity of acknowledging their reception.

I'm glad my letters interest and please you so much. But I believe you think yours don't give me near that amount of pleasure that mine does you. You know not with what anxiety and pleasure I look forward to their reception, and with how full of gladness and love my heart is made by a perusal of them.

You say "You don't believe I have any idea how much you do love me". Can't I form an idea from the love I bear you? Do I not love you *dearly*? Alva, you *must* know I do. This heart *could not* love more true.

Don't think any longer that there is any point about which I'm dissatisfied, for there is not, if so I would tell you. I'm sorry what I said gave you so much uneasiness of mind. It was all unintentionally done.

I gave you my only reason for saying what I did in my last. I know you've used every effort in your power to see me; consequently I am satisfied. Your letters are all very explicit and satisfactory indeed all that I could wish or ask.

With pleasure I accept the ring with all your love. I like it *very* much. It is a neat piece of work; something different from anything I've seen. I intend sending you some token of my love and remembrance soon. I wanted to April Fool you with it but was not prepared. Babe fooled me completely on the lst. She wrote some poetry, put in an envelope and gave it to a young man who is boarding here going to school, to give to me, pretending like he brought it from the Office. So soon as I read it, I accused him of writing it, and told him I knew it was from no one but a "Shin plaster". They teased me very much and it was several days before I found, out Babe was the Sender.

You asked me to tell you who I thought wrote my Valentine. You know very well who I suspicion; but *you* say you didn't write any. Now I always believe all you tell me. So I think some one else wrote it and you *sent* it. I'm confident you selected or made the poetry. Am I not right?

I'm glad you soldiers have such interesting amusements to wear away the dull monotonous camp life. I like to hear of you exhibiting such spirits of cheerfulness. I read today a letter in the Telegraph some one in your portion of the Army who gave a very interesting and amusing account of the battles fought there during the snow storm last month.

We heard from Bro yesterday, he is in Greenville, Tenn., thinks that Army will be sent back to Va. this spring. I hope so at least, as they prefer it to Tenn.

The Spring campaign will no doubt soon open and I do hope our Army will never invade Yankee soil any more. It seems we never meet with so much success as when we fight on the defensive.

Will you excuse half sheet this time? I will do better next time. There is preaching at the school-house today, and as I want to go, I've had to write in haste.

My school is still increasing. I have forty seven. Cousin Eliza Hall assists me. I will write again soon. The family sends love. I remain as ever your admirer.

Mag

Camp "Jennie Hart" Wright's Brigade
Madison Run April 22nd 1864
Dearest Mag,

It seems almost an age since I last wrote and I have not heard a single word from you yet. As my mess mate has gone to Richmond, I am indeed "deeply, darkly, desperately blue", and I will to night, try and write. If I do not get a letter tomorrow I will, indeed, begin to despond. Mag, you've spoiled me by writing to me so often, and if you don't continue I am afriad I will go cra _ ing you to please write to me oftener, for awhile, at least until the coming campaign commences. I knew, that when the campaign commenced, I would have to give up the pleasure of receiving your dear, dear letters; but the nearer the time approaches, the more I hate it. I try and not suffer my mind to dwell on such melancholly subjects; but I know also too well (from sad experience) that all correspondence with those we love must necessarily cease. If our present relations were not as they are, this affection would even *then*, be painful; but it is infinitely more so now. I will try, however, and bear it the best I can; but I assure you the period, during which I fail to receive your ever welcome, happiness-creating letters, will be one of loneliness and melancholly to me. If you should fail to hear from me often, do not attribute the delay to any want of sincerity or any neglect; for believe me Mag the only true happiness I experience is in corresponding with you. As in all probability it will be a long long time before we can *exchange* letters again, will you think me presumptuous if I write you little *book* to criticise during leisure hours? ---- but I forget I am no "Author". I mean a *long letter*. In every letter receive I find something to make me love you more and more. You are a true and noble woman, and I cannot be happy without you. (I don't flatter). When you said, "I know of nothing antagonistic to our love, if so, I would tell you", you courced such nobleness of character such unmistakeable sincerity, as to perfectly satisfy me (*if I were ever dissatisfied*), and I am more content and happy, with one exception, I desire *so much* to see you. I will not ask you to remove that, for I know you can not; if you could, I would apply, to you, immediately for a furlough, and I believe too I would be more successful than I was in my last effort. You would "*approve*" it would you not? If not I should have to put you on the list with Lt. Gen. A. P. Hill as a *very* cruel "*general*". You *officers* ought to remember that a year seems to us an *age*. Truly it seems to me as if I had not seen you in two or three years; but hope on hope ever. If what I have written causes you to think me melancholly, *you* are to blame not I. You made me so, by not writing often.

I wish I could write you an entire letter without a single reference to military affairs; but being directly in the war, how can I do otherwise than sometimes displease you with a recital of events which to you have long since become trite and common. I too, must say, that the description of our *every day* transactions are to *me* very uninteresting; but there *are* episodes, (of very rare occurence) which interest us very much, to a description of such, I would now ask your *"prayerful attention"*. I ought not to have said that, I mean, careful attention.

'Twouldn't do to scratch it out it would *spoil the paper*. Well, I will commence. Since I last wrote, I have again attended (*invited by special orders*) another *ball*. Of course I enjoyed myself if "amazingly", as a *silent observer*. I could *look* at the ladies as much as I pleased, but dared not speak to them no not I. It is indeed quite humiliating; but I know if I can not speak to the "F., F. Vs" of Virginia, I *can* write to you, which is I assure you far more preferable, than a week's "confab", with the most intelligent, most beautiful lady in Virginia. I am ashamed to say it' but I am afraid I haven't that charity for the fair sex, that I ought to have. Not that the ladies of Virginia fail to posses those virtues which are necessary to constitute a perfect lady; but being *common* soldiers, and not having "good clothes", we do not feel ourselves *"fit"* to appear in ladies society. In other words, gold lace, stars and bars, *outrank* us. I know that grades of distinction in the *army* are absolutely necessary to the preservation of order and discipline; but I think at private parties all such ought to be laid aside.

Another tournament, given by Genl. A. P. Hill and staff, has taken place since I last wrote. It was conducted on a different plan from the former one, of which I gave you description. There were about thirty "Knights", from our corps only; who contested for the prizes. The first prize was awarded to Capt. Luckie of the Third Georgia. At first it was a "tie" between Capt. Luckie and a Virginian (courier for Genl. Hill). A young lady hearing the decision of the judges, remarked "now the contest is fairly between Georgia and Virginia, we will *see* who is successful". She *did* see, that Georgia was again successful in the *tournament*, as she is *always* in every other contest. There was a very large crowd present. Quite a number of generals witnessed the contest. Lt. Genl. Hill headed the list. Next came Maj. Genl. Anderson[8], Maj. Genl. Heeth[9], Maj. Genl. Johnson[10], Brig. Genl. Wright[11], Brig. Genl. Davis (nephew to the President), Brig.Genl. Thomas[12], Brig. Genl. Perry[13], Brig. Genl. Walker[14] and Brig. Genl. Kirkland[15]. A large number of Cols., Lt. Cols., Majs. Capts. Lts. and soldiers composed the audience. A few ladies, only were present. Instead of the victors crowning the ladies on the field, that ceremony was to take place at the coronation ball given a few nights afterwards. We for a wonder were spared the disagreeable necessity of attending. I will now dismiss the tournament, and commence a new subject, which will far more interest you, and show that our Brigade is improving in "morale" as well as in Chivalry.

The day appointed by Pres. Davis[16] and recommended by our beloved commander, Genl. Lee, for fasting and prayer, was, I am proud to say, properly observed in our brigade. Prayer meeting was held twice, and two excellent sermons delivered on that day. The most appropriate and interesting was delivered at eleven oclock, by Mr. Cook, chaplain of the second Ga. Battalion, from the text found in Second Corinthians, Seventh chapter and fourteenth verse. It was an able effort, and I have no doubt, produced great good. A very large crowd was present all seeming to manifest great interest in the

---

[8] Major General Richard Heron Anderson, CSA.

[9] Major General Henry Heth. CSA.

[10] Believed to be Major General Bushrod Rust Johnson, CSA.

[11] Brigider General Ambrose Ransom Wright.

[12] Brigider General Bryan Morel Thomas, CSA.

[13] Brigider General William Flank Perry, CSA.

[14] Believed to be Brigider General Reuben Lindsay Walker, CSA.

[15] Brigider General William Whedbee Kirkland, CSA.

[16] President Jefferson Davis, CSA.

services. At the close of the services quite a number desired an interest in the prayers of the people of God. Since that time I have seen Mr. Hyman, a baptist minister of Thomas Ga. Brig., baptize and receive into the baptist church, nine of our best soldiers. One of the number was from my company. On the night of the same day, quite a number were *sprinkled into* the Methodist church. Although all the chaplains in our brigade, are of the Methodist denomination, all who profess conversion do not join the Methodist church. The good work is still progressing. Our chaplains are doing all in *their* power. God help them.

I must again recur to that disagreeable camp description; but as I have something to tell you, which probably you do not know, I will reconsider the wish I made in the beginning of this letter. A few days since we received orders from Genl. Lee, that "should any of the brave soldiers of this army be so unfortunate as to fall into the hands of the enemy, they should not tell to what brigade, division or corps they belonged; but simply give their names, company and regiment; also that prisoners should not talk with each other in reference to anything connected with the army". Upon the reception of these orders we immediately set our wits to work and soon decided that we were to be reinforced from some point. Subsequent events have proven that we were right in our conjectures. From all accounts Longstreet's corps is undoubtedly at Charlottesville, about twenty five miles from this place. There being so much uncertainty about the time we will move we will, in al probability, not be able to see each other in a long time.

This is a beautiful day and the singing of the birds, and the warm sunshine sensibly remind us that Spring with its "bloom and beauty" has again come, cheering and enlivening us with its gentle influence. You wouldn't think that it was a source of much pleasure to *us*, when it is so surely the forerunner of trouble and hardship; but we know we have to suffer and we are anxious for it to be over with as soon as possible. While I am writing I can see several groups of boys enjoying themselves in different ways. Some are playing ball, some *base* (I don't know any other way to spell it) and some engage in that game the ladies generally play, "Graces". Imagine some one attempting to write while surrounded by two or three hundred noisey soldiers, and you have pictured my situation exactly. How can you then, expect me to write anything interesting? I will keep on until I finish this sheet anyhow.

I enclose a specimen of Mr. Hindells (our leader) arrangement of music. I think it is a most beautiful duet, and hope you will be pleased with it. I only wish it were something worth sending. You and Miss Samantha must sing it for me when I *next* see you. Please accept it.

There is no doubt now that our brigade will in a few days be reinforced by the addition of the sixty third Georgia Regiment, for some time stationed at Savannah, and the tenth Georgia Battalion. I hope they will come. Genl. Wright is entitled to a larger command.

I have been looking for a letter from you for several days and you cannot imagine how uneasy my not receiving one, has made me. I made *lots* of excuses for their delay. Sometimes I feared you might be sick; at others, that probably Jack might be at home, and that you were waiting to write by him or that probably you had written by mail and your letter had been lost. I know you have written; but why I have not received it is as yet unsolved. You know not with what anxiety I have awaited its arrival. If I do not get an answer tomorrow, I will write anyhow, for I know *you* will not think me impertinent. I *hope* you have not been sick, if so please accept my heartfelt sympathy, and the wish that you may speedily recover. I am almost afraid to get a letter, for fear something *serious* has happened to your or your Father's family. It may be though, that you have been made the happy recipient of some great pleasure; if so, I hope you experienced *great* happiness in its 'reception.

My mess mate (Mr. Morgan[17]) has returned from Richmond, having "lots" to tell; but it is all about his "Emma". I almost envy his pleasure experienced in her presence; for I too am, *you know not how anxious*, to see a certain "Maggie" in Georgia. Yesterday evening he

---

[17] Believed to be Adrian S. Morgan, later appointed 2nd Lieutenant

received a most beautiful tobacco pouch from a young lady in Warrenton Ga., whom he has never seen. He some time ago wrote her a letter acknowledging the receipt of a pair of socks bearing her name, and returning his thanks. The tobacco pouch was the only reply he has ever received.

Millwood, Georgia
April 22th 1864
Dear Alva
Last mail day, Saturday, just as we were in the act of starting off to church I recd. your last letter; also one from my good Aunt whom I visited last summer and whom I hadn't heard from in a long time. I read the contents of each going on to church. So *much* pleasure at once.

In the evening after I came home, according to a previous promise I went over to see Miss Mollie Deaton who is a near neighbor of ours, her father having moved to the place where Capt. Collins lived when you were here. He is now a Chaplain in the Army of Tenn. His family resides in Perry[18]. But more concerning my visit. I had scarcely time to pass the usual compliments with the family, however, before Miss M. discovered my new rings you sent, saying "Oh what nice rings you have! Where did you get them? Who made them? Did your sweetheart give them to you?" What do you suppose my reply was? It was this- A friend. "Yes" she said, "a very dear one I guess". She teased me some time, thinking she would find out the sender; but her efforts were all in vain.

I love Mollie, and would make her my confidant; provided I didn't have a grown sister. She is indeed an amiable young lady; and I've often said the prettiest I ever saw. She frequently asks me who is it in the army that I claim the affections of. She was not acquainted in this neighborhood before the war; consequently she can't even guess correctly who my "Spicy" (her own term) is.

---

[18] Perry, Georgia

With pleasure I accept the very nice ring and all your love, with the belief that you will prove true to her who has rec'd it. I will wear it and ever remember him who has won my confidence and entire affections.

Sure enough as you anticipated I haven't a ring suitable to give you, but as you so much desire it, I enclose one within. It is very slender and I fear will not wear long, though it is the best I can do now. Perhaps when you visit I will have one more suitable. I have tried to swap it for a plain one, but all seem to prefer as well as myself, those kind. So I couldn't succeed.

You say "I may destroy, give away or keep the first ring you sent". That reminds me of what Sis said when she presented you with the gloves. Whenever you see me, I guess you'll see that ring, as I'm wearing both and will continue to.

Sis told me to tell you "that she never----- her intended being one of the unfortunate who has fallen in battle", but you needn't believe the half of it. I know there is a certain Mississippi soldier whom she doesn't dislike much. I told her I intended to contradict her message or at least to correct it.

We are expecting Joe Graham home every day. I read a letter from Bro a few days since, which was written to a friend. He said Joe had made an application for a furlough, and he thought would be successful. They are now at or near Bristol. It is generally conceded, that Longstreet's Corps, will go back to Virginia this spring and is now-------

(Incomplete letter from Margaret L. Cone to Alva B. Spencer)

Wrights' Brigade
Madison Run Virginia

May 2nd 1864

Dear Maggie,

Yesterday, your most interesting letter of the 22nd ultimo enclosing a nice ring was received and I now return you my *most sincere* thanks. It suits me finely.

I am almost sick to day, and I feel *very* little like writing. I never in my life had such a bad cold. I will try however and write today, for fear I might be less able, here-after. I hope I shall feel better tomorrow.

We have just received orders to report at brigade head quarters. We, I presume, are to play for some "May party". Have you attended any? I don't suppose I can write but a few more lines before I will have to leave. Should we attend a party, I will give you an account of it. You, no doubt, think me foolish in attending this party, if I am sick. But you must recollect that we are bound to go and come at our commanders *bidding*. As our leader is now calling us to get ready, I must close until I return, when I hope I will feel better.

I have returned from the "Pic Nic", and as I expected, I am not all benefitted by the trip. I suppose you would like to know something of the party. Well, I haven't much to say about that; for it was evidently a complete failure. There were only three or four ladies present, and about double that number of gentlemen. We remained only a short time after our arrival. As we anticipated, it was at Montpelier, rather noted as being the burial place of President Madison. Like most places in Virginia, it has felt the influence of this ravaging war; but still it is a most beautiful place. I enjoyed myself finely in going over its extensive grounds. The mansion is situated upon a pretty high place, and the view in front is most enchanting. Far away to the north may be seen the "Blue Ridge Mountains" rising in majestic beauty. When we look in other directions, the scenery is indeed beautiful, varied by hill and vale seasoning, with cattle and the beauties of spring. I think it by far, the most beautiful place I have seen in Virginia. On our return a terrible storm arose, giving us all a good *ducking*, which by the way, was not very well for me. When I arrived in camp, what was my surprise to find my tent blown down, and my blankets perfectly saturated with the rain. You can imagine what *pleasant, comfortable* sleep I will have tonight. I am used to such tho', therefore don't feel much apprehension.

3rd May-

I slept finely last night. You do not believe it possible for one to *sleep finely* with wet blankets. I know you do not; but when one is worn out with the hardships of the day, he can rest anywhere and under any circumstances. This morning, we received orders to send all tents to the rear, so I expect we will have to try it out doors awhile. I have been expecting it some time, so I am not at all surprised. Everything indicates a move of some sort *soon*. I am just as willing for it to come now as ever. I expect I am just as well *prepared* now as I will be.

Yesterday evening upon my arrival at camp, I found that one of my company had just returned from home bringing me lots of good things; so I hope to live well for a day or two at least. Anything in the eatable line from home is always acceptable I assure you. I have been very fortunate in *that respect* this winter. If I didn't get a furlough, I received boxes from home; which was, you know, better than not receiving either.

I am truly glad that you received the last ring I sent you, and that you are so well pleased with it. I greatly feared it would be lost. I hesitated sometime whether to send it by mail or wait and bring it to you. I am glad now, I adopted the course I did.

We will have brigade drill this morning, so I will have to *stop again*. I will send it of tomorrow anyhow. I am almost ashamed to send you this letter; but under the circumstances you must excuse me this time. Will you not?

Tell Miss Sis she needn't think to fool me by saying she has no sweet heart. If she hasn't one I will give her one. She told me the same story when I last saw her. I believed her *then*; but now *you* say she is not entirely indifferent to a certain Mississippi gentleman, so I am at a loss *what* to think of her. Just tell her I shall not be surprised at any day to hear of her being Mrs. _____.

You say you've heard only two reasons assigned by the ladies, for rejecting the suits of the soldiers. As to the objection being made to receiving addresses by letter, I have before told you that I too should prefer it otherwise; but it must be recollected that a soldier cannot *always be* where he most desires. Cannot they wave that slight objection when they know the character of the addresser? And it is to be presumed that no one who is not well acquainted with a lady would make such a declaration. As to their being afraid of their letters being shown, I think that is no excuse at all. Is it not known to all that love affairs are too sacred to be exposed to the view of others? I think they are unnecessarily alarmed on that subject. If these are their only excuses, I honestly think they treat the soldiers very unkindly. I am truly glad to know, Mag, that such fears had so little influence with *you*. If you did urge such objections, you believed me when I pledged myself true, and made me the happiest being in the world. Oh, how I do long to prove to you that I am not unworthy the confidence and affection you have bestowed upon me. I think of you all the time, and my love grows with my thoughts. I hope to see you soon and then I will tell you more than I can write. Mag, should you hear any lady objecting to a ----, and if she knows him personally for the above reasons; just tell her they are no reasons at all. This is honestly my opinion.

When I last saw you, you, spoke in very high terms of Miss Mollie; but at the time she was sick, or I should then have solicited her acquaintance. I should like very much to see her. Maybe I will. You are not afraid to risk me falling in love with her, are you? I *shall not promise you* to be uninfluenced; for, from your description, she must ----. You will give me a trial tho', will you not?

I wrote you in my last that I had visited Jack and Joe. They then told me that Joe had sent forward his application for a furlough. I hope ere this reaches you, they may both be enjoying the pleasures of home. Jack told me he didn't (know) when he should apply. I think his time *ought* to have come long before this. If he succeeds in getting his commission, I think he will be much more fortunate, than if he could get several furlough I hope he may succeed. But you know it is much easier to get into service than to get out. I have found it so since I've been in service.

We are going to have a grand May dinner in our house today. We will have corn bread, meat, peas, syrup, coffee (sweetened) and cakes. Don't you think that will do for camp life? But nearly all of it came from home. If we could always draw such from the Government we would get along finely.

I enclose a piece of cedar from the grave of Madison. I do not know the emblem, but if it is *good*, I agree with it, if not, accept it merely as a curiosity. I would like to give you a description of his tomb; but I am not at all competent, mentally or physically. It was plain, but beautiful. I hope I will be able to write you something interesting next time. If I am sick I shall always write, if only a few lines. My respects to all the family. Miss Sis & my friends all. I will write again soon.

Remember me as ever yours devotedly,
Alva

Millwood, Georgia
May 13th 1864
Dear Alva,

Yours of a late date was rec'd. a few days since and I would have answered at an earlier day but have had no opportunity of sending a letter off.

I too had begun to wonder what could be the cause of your long silence, but all was explained when I rec'd. your last. I can't see why letters are so long delayed on the way. I rarely get one under twelve days after it is written and I think mine are much longer going to you.

As yet we have mail but once a week unless some of the neighbors go out to Vienna after it, which is not done often. That looks as if the people here are not very much interested about the war and their friends, doesn't it? Well, in truth Pa and Mr. Henry are all that ever do feel deeply enough interested to search for it, although all are very anxious to hear the news, but not enough so to trouble themselves by going after it. When we get letters, it matters not how anxious we are to reply, have to wait a week unless by chance we have an opportunity of mailing elsewhere. But as the campaign has commenced, I hope better arrangements will be made. By the kindness of Mrs. Roberts (one of my patrons), I am furnished with the Telegraph every morning which she receives the ever evening. It is always thankfully rec'd.

We are awaiting with much anxiety and fear to hear the full results of the late engagement in Virginia. Not that we fear our army will be unable to cope with the enemy in his strategic movements, for we have already learned that in every effort so far he has been foiled and beaten back but the catalogue of our killed and wounded we fear will make us very sad to read over. We are grieved to hear that Gen. Longstreet was wounded but hope he will recover, that his wound may not prove fatal as did Gen. Jackson's. I haven't seen but a few private telegrams. One of those was from Gen. Wright to his family. It will doubtless be several days yet before we hear from the 18th, how terrible the suspense! A few days ago we rec'd. a letter from Jack in which he said you had been to see him. I reckon you didn't see cousin John as he was in Lynchburg when we last heard. I know the boys were glad to see you. Jack said you were looking better than he ever saw you, in cheerful spirit and confident of success.

Last Sabbath Rev. A. C. Dayton, a refugee from Nashville, Tenn., preached at our church. I was much pleased with the discourse. I have heard him two or three times before. He is president of the college in Perry. You may perhaps have seen him and read some of his writings. He is an unyielding baptist and his lady a Presbyterian. The people are much pleased with him in Perry.

It is now the lovely month of May, and everything is smiling with the beauties of Spring.

A few evenings since I made a bouquet and put in press, a part of which I enclose within. They are some of my most favorite flowers. I don't know the emblem, therefore they are not sent. I merely send them because I like them and thinking *you would be pleased even* to see some flowers from Georgia.

In your last you asked me to send you my ambrotype, I have two, but neither of them I think resembles the original much, and when I give you one I want it to be a good one. I will

promise however to have one taken, if possible this year and give you when I see you.

My school will be out in three weeks. I shall be glad and sorry too, glad to have the cares of school off of my mind; but will hate to bid the scholars adieu. Today little Kate brought me such nice strawberries. I had enough to divide with all the girls and brought some home to Minnie.

Since I last wrote Pa has been very sick, but is now rapidly improving. Eliza and Babe indeed all send their respects and best wishes. With a hope of hearing from you soon, I remain yours devotedly.

Mag

P,S. I shall be pleased to receive the "little book or long letter" you have proffered to write. I think 'I shall be much pleased with the piece of music you sent.

Mag

Front lines at N. Virginia
Nine miles north Richmond
May 30th 1864
My dear Mag,

A long, long time has elapsed since I last wrote, and I know you must have thought strange of my delay. I trust, however, all uneasiness will be removed when you fully ascertain the cause.

On the 4th of this month we started from our encampment at Madison Station to meet the enemy. Fortunately our brigade was not in any actual engagement. Some few men killed and wounded on the skirmish line. The slaughter of the enemy in the "Wilderness" was immense. The battle was fought in a wilderness indeed no artillery being used except on the left of our line under Ewell[19]. I inquired very particularly about the causualties in Wofford's Brigade; but could hear of none of your relations being hurt. I hope they are all safe. You've no doubt heard from them ere this.

Grant finding that he could do nothing in the "Wilderness", commenced moving his army towards our right in the direction of Fredericksburg, hoping I've no doubt to flank Genl. Lee; but he was handsomely foiled by Genl. R. H. Anderson, our former division commander, at that time commanding Longstreet's Corps, whom, I forgot to mention, as being among the wounded at the "Wilderness". Our brigade didn't get into any regular engagement at that point either. The were skirmishing all the time, tho', and a good many were killed & wounded. Genl. Wright's horse was killed. After remaining in line of battle several days we were sent from the left of our line to the extreme right. At that point our brigade fought Wright's Yankee brigade losing nearly two hundred men. The enemy were badly whipped, losing a good many prisoners and several stands of colors. Jno. Hooks some relation of Miss Bettie Hooks, was wounded, and died a short while afterwards. He died on or near the field consequently I didn't see him. I only heard from him through some of his company. My company lost six or eight of wounded and

---

[19] General Richard Stoddert Ewell, CSA

one killed. We remained in this position a day or two when Grant again commenced moving to our right. We marched from our breastworks to the South Anna where we established our line. Our brigade occupied a very unenviable position I assure you. Our works could be enfiladed from two or three different ways. The Yankees amused themselves considerably in shelling us, but through God's protection very few were killed or wounded. I was never before in such a furious shelling. Genl. Wright had another horse wounded. In a few days, we again moved to our right in the direction of the Peninsula. The day we left our works, some thirty or more prisoners were captured by our brigade. The *all* say they are heartily tired of charging our works and don't intend to attempt it any more. Their losses in the recent engagement must have been dreadful. In front of some of the works on our line, they were literally "crossed and piled". Their losses in the recent engagements must have been fifty or sixty thousand.

To attempt to give you an idea of our present position, would be fruitless. I am completely *lost*. I don't know anything at all about the Geography of the country. I only know we are in line of battle about nine miles north of Richmond and not very far from Mechanicsville. Our brigade occupies a splendid position, and I can but believe, will through God's assistance, be entirely successful. Canonading is now going on, on our right. We expect an engagement soon.

As Grant is considerably nearer Richmond now than when he first crossed the "Rapid Ann", I'm afraid *some* of the people at home will think that Genl. Lee is *outflankd, out-generaled*, whipped. Let me tell you that is all entirely a mistake. Our troops were never in better spirits or more confident of success. They only await the advance of the enemy. I think none need feel any fears in reference to *this* army. I hope and confidently believe all will be well. I believe there is a Divine Providence who watches over us and will bless us and protect us.

Today we heard of Genl. Johnston's victory in the west and I'm confident that fact will greatly increase the courage and determination of our troops. That is the only point we fear. I do hope they and the whole Confederate army may be successful in the approaching struggles, and that God will crown our efforts with a speedy, happy lasting peace. If successful I really believe this will be the last year of the war.

On the march from the South Anna river to this place I had the happy pleasure of receiving your long looked for letter. You know not how happy it made me and how my heart leaped for joy when our Post Master handed me your last. I knew it as soon as I looked at it. 'Tis said that "*absence* conquers love"; but I'm now prepared to contradict it. I *know* the *absence* of your letters has caused me not to love you less but more. I do hope we may be able to hear from each other more frequently, since we have moved so much nearer Richmond. I return you my sincere thanks for the nice boquet and verses. You say you do not know the emblem, neither do I, but I know the fact that *you* sent it said that is enough for me. I am peculiarly fond of flowers, especially when presented by those we love. I intend to keep it so long as a piece remains. I almost envy you the pleasure you derive in attending to your flower garden. I wish I could assist you. I expect you are now enjoying the strawberries. I do wish I could get some. That's child like, isn't it? I received a letter from Mother the other day telling me that, as I couldn't be there to help them eat them, she would preserve them for me, so if I live and nothing happens, I will get some after all. They will be *almost* as good as if they were ripe and fresh.

I think you are too hasty in your decision concerning the ambrotype. I think *I* ought to be the judge as to whether it resembles the original. I don't recollect of ever having an ambrotype of myself that I thought resembled the original, and Mag, I believe *you* are the same way. You *know* I *very* much desire your picture; but if you had rather not send it now, I will not insist; but I shall expect it when I next see you. If I can't see *you*, I would like very much to see your *representative*. You must know 'twould cheer me in many a lonely hour.

I'm very sorry to hear of your Father's illness. I hope he has ere this fully recovered, and is able, again to commence his good works in your neighborhood. I honestly believe that if he were not in the neighborhood, the society would be far different. He is indeed the soul of the neighborhood. Do you expect to teach school again? I will write again soon. Please write often whether you receive my letters or not. My respects to your Father's family, Eliza, Mrs. H., Miss Sis & all my friends.

I remain as ever yours devotedly,

Alva

At home, Monday
May 30th 1864
Dear Alva,

Saturday, your welcome letter of the 3rd was rec'd. It had been some time since I had heard from you, though I could very easily account for the delay, as the army has been marching and fighting all this month, and part of the time communications cut off between Petersburg and Richmond.

We have a letter from Brother dated 17th he was safe up to that time. None of the Co. killed but a few slightly wounded. He thinks the decisive battle has not yet been fought. It seems that the enemy are making stronger efforts to get Richmond than ever before. I have no fears of his being successful, too many unsuccessful attempts have been made. We have the ultimate confidence in our army of VA. believe it will do its whole duty. Gen. Johnson, it is thought, will fall back to Atlanta. The women and children have been ordered to leave the city. The people seem to have no fears but what this movement will "turn out for the best". All have great confidence in Johnson.

I have more fears that the 20,000 Yankee prisoners at Anderson (which is only 28 or 30 miles from here) will make their escape, than anything else. The force we have to guard them, is thought by some not strong enough. I don't know the number of troops we have there.

Col. Persons who commands the post has recently written to the Secretary of War for more troops. I hope a sufficient number will be sent him.

Gov. Brown has ordered all the Militia to report at Atlanta, and all civil officers under the age of 50. Pa was 50 in Feb. last. So the call does not quite reach him. The Militia of this county left one week ago. Uncle Thomas Cone was one of the number. I felt a little sorry for some of them, as their farms required their attention, more now than any other time during the year. But the most of these men have been subject to conscription for a year or more consequently they don't deserve sympathy. At this critical time every one should be at his post of duty.

Joe Graham's furlough was disapproved, therefore, we do not expect him or Brother home before next winter. It really seems very hard if it is fiar for so long a time to elapse before we can see them.

Since I last wrote I have been very sick, and am not well yet. I was taken with chill and fever the next day after I wrote you and continued to have them for several days during which time Samantha taught school for me. Last week I dismissed my school. Ma advised me to do so, as I was unable to teach and only liked two weeks of teaching out the term and Samantha didn't wish to have charge of the school any longer.

I think I had light chill and fever yesterday. My head ached very bad all day. I feel very well today, but tomorrow I am almost certain will be sick as I have them every other day. If I would take physic[20] well, I wouldn't hate so bad to be sick. Ma has to almost whip me every time I'm sick about taking physic. I know I'm very foolish about it, but to save my life I can't help it.

We have no physicians left here but Dr. Cross and he has almost quit the practice. Dr. Pattishaw our best physician had to leave with the militia. I don't know how the neighborhood can do without him. I hated to see him leave worse than all the "malish".

---

[20] Believed to be a laxative.

I haven't attended a single May party. I'm sorry you were sick and couldn't enjoy yourself better at yours. I shan't be surprised to hear that you were very sick after being caught in such a rain and being almost sick any way. I hope not though. You said you would write soon, so I hope to get a letter this week.

I shall not object to you seeing Mollie when you visit, no, but I tell you time, "You had better not fall in love for some one *might* put a spider in your dumpling", though if you do not become captivated, I shall think it very strange. For I know you will be obliged to confess that she is a beautiful young lady.

We have some ripe fruit now, plums, mulberries, strawberries, raspberries etc. I ought not talk about them, ought I? as you are deprived of such luxuries. I have been fishing once but caught no fish. There are but few fish in the creeks.

When I get well, Mrs. Felden, Samantha and myself are going to Cuthbert, though we will not remain long, not more than 10 or 12 days. I'm afraid to stay longer for I don't wish to be sick from home. Indeed we couldn't make a long visit as Mrs. F. will want us to accompany her back. We will have no opportunity for seeing the Yankee prisoners as we will get in the train at Montezuma and go through Camp Anderson. I'm so afraid of a Yankee, I don't know whether I want to see them or not. You must excuse these hastily written lines, I will do better next time. The emblem of ---- is think of me very good, and I accept.

I remain yours affectionately,
Mag

Millwood, Georgia
June 21st 1864
Dear Alva,

A few days since your most welcome letter of 30th ult. was rec'd., and contents read with much delight. It seemed almost an age since I last heard from you, indeed I had begun to despair, though, of course, I could easily account for your long silence, knowing the army has been continually marching or fighting for a considerably length of time, but still I dident know whether you were one of the fortunate or unfortunate, consequently was very anxious to hear. I am glad you have been so much blessed thus far, and hope may continue to be.

We have letter from Jack of ---- up to which time, himself and Joe were safe. Bat Cone a cousin of ours, was killed. We are pained to hear of his death, he was a mess mate of Jack's and a most excellent soldier.

Riley Hooks was taken prisoner. It seems to me death would almost be preferable to a prisoner's life, though I know life is very sweet; but the horrible treatment one receives during the confinement, and being debarred the priviledge of hearing from home only once perhaps in six months is enough to kill, and doubtless has many hundreds.

John is yet in hospital at Lynchburg, has been quite sick but was improving at last accounts. He is rather desponding about the war, says there is no prospect of a termination of hostilities soon or late. I am going to tease him when I next write him. He used to laugh so much at me whenever I expressed any fears in reference to our fate. I have not lost hopes of a better day coming. Gen. Timmbs says this, "the present is the brightest day which has ever dawned upon our Confederacy". But Gov. Brown and Mr. Stephens would have us believe it is about the darkest. My motto is fight on fight ever rather than submit to Yankee rule and oppression.

A great many refugees are coming in here from the upper portion of the state. I don't think the Yankees will ever want to come down this far, if so, we are fortunately situated, are we not?

Dooly is a great place these times, better once though, than never, the *Houstonites* say.

We have been having a great deal of rain for the past two weeks which has almost destroyed the whole wheat crop through this section. Pa says not one in fifty will be able to save seed. We have been more fortunate than a good many as our best wheat was saved before the rain set in. The corn crop will not be near so good. The water courses are very high. Pa says there is much uneasiness among the people in reference to the prospect of provisions for the next year.

I don't expect to teach school any more. I invariably get sick, and Ma says I shouldn't teach any more. I am very willing too, My health has improved considerably since I last wrote. We will go to Randolph as soon as the water falls, though I will write again before that time. I guess we will go out the lst of July. You continue to write we will remain only a week or so. All is well and send much love.

Yours devotedly,
Mag

Petersburg
June 26th '64
Dearest Maggie,

Yesterday evening after I was almost exhausted attending the wounded, your last most interesting letter of the lst inst. was received and I assure you it exerted a most revivifying influence. Since we came to the South side of the James river, our communication has been so often disturbed, that I had almost despaired of receiving your dear letters or of writing myself. Communication is now cut off, so I'm afraid you will not receive this in some time if ever. I will write, tho, as it will somewhat ease my anxiety. In other words I will feel better.

I am truly sorry you have been sick, but hope you've ere this entirely recovered and completed with much pleasure your anticipated visit to Cuthbert. I hope however you will not be so unfortunate as you were before.

I am considerably better than I was before, but still very weak and hardly able to keep up. I hope we will have a little rest soon.

You will see by the above caption that we are considerably further South than when I last wrote. Our brigade has been in two fights recently, losing a good many men. About fifty killed, and nearly two hundred wounded. Our company has been very fortunate indeed. Our 3rd Lt. McWhorter[21] and one man killed[22], one wounded[23] were the casualties in the company.

As usual they fought in open field. They had to leave their fortifications and flank the enemy from the Petersburg and Weldon R.R. They captured several stands of colors, about 2,000 prisoners, five pieces of artillery, and drove them from several lines of entrenchment. Our brigade was in advance & did the greater part of the fighting. They were *supported* by other troops of our division; but they are entitled to *all* the honor. The Virginia papers however, give all the praise to Mahone's brigade (Va.). I expect you will see accounts of it soon. I believe my account is the more correct & the most impartial.

How long this kind of (war) will continue no one knows, but I hope it will stop soon, a great many of our men are becoming sick and broken down. One side or the other will have to stop pretty soon or each army be very much reduced.

Three cheers for the "Milish". They have had quite a turning out in our county, too. Nearly all have gone.

I should like very much to have some of that good fruit; but I suppose if I *can't*, I *can't*, that's all. I want you to enjoy it, tho'. I have had a few vegetables since we came to this place. The people here are very kind indeed. They visit our hospitals with refreshments every evening. They are doing all they can for the soldiers. They no doubt feel very much relieved; for they expected ere this to have seen the Yankee army quartered in Petersburg. Love to all. Excuse this short unsatisfactory letter. Write often to your devoted.

Alva

---

[21] 3rd Lt. Robert P. McWhorter, Killed on picket duty in Petersburg June 19, 1864

[22] Private Hardee (or Hardy) Lanier, Killed in Petersburg June 22, 1864

[23] Private John L. McGuire, Killed in Petersburg, June 22, 1864

CHAPTER FIVE

1864

July through December

In this second half of our 1864 letters, Margaret takes a train trip to visit relatives in Cuthbert, Ga. On the return trip the train breaks down for several hours leaving the passengers temporary stranded in the woods. After the arrival of another engine, the trip continued only to have the train derail a short time later close to Andersonville Prison. Knowing of Margaret's great fear of seeing a Yankee soldier, one can imagine her feelings "trapped" in the woods like this. Union Lt. Colonel Henry Pleasants, of the 48th Pennsylvania Infantry, came up with the idea of digging a mine underneath the nearby Confederate camp in Petersburg, filling it with explosives and igniting a deadly charge. The 48th Pennsylvania, made up of former coal miners from Northern Pennsylvania, began digging the tunnel on June 25th and finished on July 17th. The tunnel was slightly over 500 feet in length. The plan was to blow up the camp and then charge in to kill or capture surviving Confederate troops. The result was disastrous for both sides and became known as the Battle of the Crater. Alva gives his first hand account of the Battle of the Crater, and his opinion of the first black troops they had encountered. Meanwhile, Union General William Tecumseh Sherman continues his march across Georgia.

Millwood, Georgia
July 8th 1864
Dearest Alva

As I anticipated when I last wrote, we have been out to Cuthbert, visiting our relations, and have just returned home today. I intended writing you the day before we left home, but company came in and prevented me. On that day I recd. your very interesting letter of the 17ult. I hadn't heard from you before in some time, and I must admit the reception of that letter caused me to enjoy my visit much more pleasantly than I should had I not recd. it. From the time we left home, until we started back we enjoyed ourselves very well indeed, but on our return found the trip any thing but pleasant. We got on the train at Cuthbert, when in a half mile of Dawson the engine became disabled from some cause; there we were detained three hours waiting for the arrival of another engine. At eleven oclock we left Dawson, had but a short time to run to Montezuma. When we were in sight of Camp Anderson on an embankment of ten or fifteen feet the engine ran off down the embankment and jerked all the cars off track, fortunately no one was killed, one lady was wounded by jumping out before the train stopped. The engine and wood box were broken all to pieces. Next box was turned nearly over, the others were merely thrown off track. I was never so badly frightened before. Some hollowed a "collision", others "fire"! You can imagine our feelings better than I describe them, I thought we should all be killed. Several ladies came near fainting. The Conductor soon had another engine brought to our assistance from Anderson with open cars attached. Our baggage was soon put on, which then one oclock, and I don't think the sun ever shone so warmly the gentlemen broke down brushes, which we used as a substitute for umbrellas. Don't you wish you could have seen us coming up to Anderson? I could but laugh thinking how singular we looked riding on platform, *real soldier fashion*, but we felt truly thankful that our condition was no worse. When we arrived at Anderson a passenger train was waiting for us, so we soon got aboard and in a few minutes were safe in Montezuma.

We found conveyance waiting for us, and came out as far as Miss Mat Leggett's last night, arrived home at eleven oclock safely today and you don't know how glad I am. Found all well. Crawford Graham died at Savannah the 21 ult., his body was brought home for interment.

The mother and sister are very much distressed. We recd. a letter from Brother the same day I recd. your last, dated 19th ult., he was still safe. There had been considerable fighting since that date, consequently we are very uneasy, and anxious to hear from him.

Johnston's Army has fallen back to Chattahoochee river. The Yankees have possession of Marietta and have burned the military Institute. The people think Johnston hasn't a sufficient number of troops to make a fight. I hear that Gen. Lee is driving Grant back. We have been very fearful that communication would be cut off from that army. I know the soldiers must be awfully tired and worn out marching and fighting so much, and so long.

I am sorry you are sick. You have my sympathy and the wish that you may soon recover. I hope you have ere this recd. some letters from me. I have never failed to answer every letter of yours. I have delayed writing a few days longer this time than usual because I've been from home, though I shall make up for last time now if I can, will write every week, unless I hear that communication is cut off, which I hope will never be. in your last you asked again for my typo. As I before said I have one I like well enough to give you, and if I had would be afraid to send it you by mail. I prefer to give it you when I next see you. If I were to mail it you, I think it altogether doubtful about your receiving it. You are satisfied to wait till you visit us, are you? I would like much to see you and hope you will not be disappointed in your expectations next winter. During the many pleasant hours I have enjoyed for the past week with my distant relatives and friends, you were not forgotten, My Alva, and can never be. "Tis sweet to be remembered, and thou shalt not be forgotten."

Today is mail day, I hope we will get a letter from Brother and one from you, they are always so gladly recd. and recd. with *great* pleasure.

I forgot to say anything about the Yankee prison at Anderson. We were not nearer the Stockade than the depot which is three hundred yards distant I suppose, well perhaps it may have been farther but anyway we had a plain view of the stockade as we wished. There are from 30 to 35,000 thousand Yankees there now and more are coming in daily. We were told, from 100 to 150 die daily. Gen. Winder from Richmond commands the post at this time.

Please excuse half sheets. I have confederate paper, but it doesn't write well, and I prefer this kind. All send love. I am as ever yours with the same pure love.

Mag

Fortifications, Petsbg.
July 13th 1864
Dearest Maggie,

No letter yet. Still I am doomed to sad disappointment. I hope, however, to get several at once in a few days, as the rail road communication with the South is now about established. I do anticipate *so much* pleasure. There's not an hour but that your image comes up before me, and besieged as we are, our anxiety is doubly increased. I'm so anxious to hear how your anticipated visit terminated; and everything else connected with Georgia. Since the enemy has made his appearance in our own dear State, I can't think there can be any dearth of news, and I assure you anything you may write, will interest me.

The situation of affairs around Petersburg remains about the same. Grant still continues the barbarous practice of throwing shells in the city, occupied only by defenseless women and children. He seems afraid to make an advance. So he keeps up an incessant sharp shooting, and shelling, accomplishing nothing. We have, through

Northern sources, cheering news from our army in the *United States*. What is the number of our troops there no one can tell. They were all gone before we knew anything about it. One thing certain their appearance has caused the greatest excitement throughout the whole north. I've no doubt the movement will cause a withdrawal of some portion of Grant's troops; if so quite a change will be produced, and I verily believe the war will soon come to an end. Don't you hope so?

McLean's division is now in reserve, and has been for some time. I've seen several of Co. I, and they all seemed to be very much pleased with their position. I hope they may be permitted to remain so. Jack is well & in good spirits. He as well as the balance of us, look, in military parlance "used up".

Joe Graham is at the hospital. At last accounts he was getting along finely. I suppose Jack has written you all about him.

Our brigade is now in reserve & has been for several days; but we expect to go into the work tonight or tomorrow night. How long we will remain there we can not tell; but not more than five or six days at farthest. In the way of commissary stores we are getting along pretty well, except we do not get *quite* as much as we could eat. We can make out tho'. Grant can't starve us out certain. There are now enough provisions in Richmond.& Petersburg to last the army for 12 months or more. There is no doubt of that.

I do hope I will hear from you soon. You know not how anxious I am. Please write often. (I) will (write) more after awhile. My love to all the family & friends. I remain as ever yours most devotedly,

Alva

Fortifications around Petersburg
July 21st 1864
Dearest Maggie,
More than a week has elapsed since mail communication has been established with the South, and still not a line have I received from you. One day this week I received three letters from home, of

an old date; but nevertheless interesting. If I could only hear from *you* now, I think I would be more reconciled and far better satisfied.

Last night I listened to a brass band belonging to our division. They played "Lulu is gone". As I listened to it, I could but recall to mind the time when you sang it to me upon leaving Georgia for Virginia, the scene of so many hardships and sufferings. I confess now that those words touched a tender chord in my heart, and it required my utmost energy to suppress my feelings. Whenever I hear it now, those scenes are vividly recalled to my imagination, and I can but sometimes wonder if *you* ever experience the same. Simple, though it be, I can never forget it. That tune shall always be my preference, so you can "hold yourself in readiness" to play it for me, should I be so fortunate as to see you again soon. If you have become tired of it, attribute my love for it more to the *objects* and circumstances connected with its execution, than the beauty of the tune itself. Little then did I think you and I would ever learn to love each other. Your ambiguity fooled me completely, and I could but resign myself to fate. A little more than one year ago (but it seems to me two) you remarked to me the day after I arrived at your house that "you had, the day before, seen your sweetheart, just returned home, from Virginia, on furlough". Whom did you mean? I might construe it in several different ways; consequently, I was completely bewildered, and knew not what course to pursue. Had I been as wise *then* as now, I think I would have acted quite differently. You spoke in such high terms of *the one* you had seen, I at once concluded that I, to use a *military* expression, had, "gone up the sprout". So I at once concluded it were best for me to desist from any further advances towards one, whose sunny smiles and winning ways, had so often excited my admiration and esteem. That I should now possess that love and confidence so long coveted is truly happiness beyond description. It seems to have been providentially reserved, to be bestowed amidst suffering and hardship; for at the time I received your avowal of pure disinterested love for me, I was suffering extremely from the cold of winter, so well calculated to render one despondent. That letter had quite a beneficial effect.

I have just received your most interesting letter of the 8th, and you know not with what avidity I perused its contents over and over again, it being the first in such a long, long time. Had I known you had so narrowly escaped injury, from the railroad accident, I should have been much more uneasy than ever. I am so thankful that *you* all escaped with so little injury. I know you must have enjoyed your trip in the open cars to Anderson. Had it been raining, I think you would have felt much more like a soldier. I expect if the Yankey prisoners saw you, they were secretly, very much amused at the condition of the rebels. They are not so frightful after all, are they? I don't suppose tho' your party had entirely recovered from the fear caused by the "collision" and "fire".

'Tis indeed gratifying to know that however distant I may be, I am still remembered in love, and that I am sympathized with in all the dangers and hardships of a soldier. This fact increases my love for you, and I can but think how greatly blessed I am, in the *possession* of that love. I am truly glad that thoughts of me were a source of pleasure to you in your recent visit to your relations. My greatest delight is in thinking and dreaming of *you*. May we continue to be, mutually, sources of pleasure to each other; happy ourselves and making all around us happy.

I was over to see Jack a day or two since. I found him safe and well; but, like all the balance of us, tired of this protracted campaign. His Division has been in reserve ever since the army came to this place They all seem not in the least *dissatisfied* with their position. I hope they may continue to be in reserve.

How long we will remain in this situation we cannot tell. It seems as if Grant is determined, if not driven away, to remain here all summer. I do wish this campaign would close, 'tis very disagreeable, and very unhealthy, both from *bullets* & disease. We can stand it about as well as Grant, tho'.

'Twas hoped that Early's[1] raid into Pennsylvania (about which you've already heard) would have caused a withdrawal of more of Grant's troops. So far our too sanguine hopes have been blasted.

It is now certainly known that Genl. Johnston has been relieved of his command and Genl. Hood[2] has assumed command. Hood is an excellent officer, and I've no doubt will soon relieve the downtrodden portions of our beloved state. The Yankeys are getting uncomfortably near my home and I'm extremely anxious they should be driven away as speedily as possible. They have overrun enough of our state, and I think it is now time for them to "*halt*". I received two letters from home today, and they exhibit great uneasiness lest Sherman should overrun our portion of the state. Our county is actually filled up with refugees from the northern part of Georgia. Every vacant building is occupied, rendering the necessaries of life extremely scarce & high. Already some of our frightened citizens have removed to the lower counties. I think there is no use in being in such a hurry, Sherman hasn't got Atlanta yet' nor do I believe he will. If he does succeed he will be compelled to do some very hard fighting, I'm certain. 'Twouldn't surprise me at any day to receive orders to go to Georgia to the assistance of Hood. I think if *any* ' troops are sent south, A.P. Hill's corps will go. I'm not at all anxious unless I could stop on the way *awhile*.

Finding it impossible to preserve your letters as I desired, I have taken the liberty to intrust them to the care of my sister Fannie[3]. I sent them to her, privileging her to read them. She has received them safe, and in her letter of today says, "I judge from her letters that she doesn't 'put on' in the least. I know she loves you, and I don't see how you *can help loving her*. As for me, I love her now, and long so much to see her and know her. From her letters I think she is very gentle, confiding & affectionate. This just such a *sister* as I want. Won't you write to *me alone* and tell me all about her, how she looks,

---

[1] Major General Jubal Anderson Early, CSA
[2] General John Bell Hood, CSA
[3] Julia Frances Spencer (Alva's sister)

etc.? I think of her often, and wish this *"cruel war"* would end." She says "write to me alone" because I'm in the habit of writing to the whole family in one letter. I have written her own words, verbatim. I never loved so much, as since I've been deprived the pleasure of being with her.

You do not object to the course I've pursued, do you? Although I should like *very* much to receive your ambrotype, I am willing to await your pleasure. I will try and go to see Jack tomorrow. Write often. Love to all your Father's family & our friends. Please extend my sympathy to Miss Graham & Mothers in the loss of *her* relative.

I remain as ever yours, devotedly,
Alva

Petersburg, Virginia
August 6th 1864
Dearest Maggie,
Yesterday I again received another of your most interesting letters & I needn't again tell you with what mingled emotions of love and pleasure I read it. I am truly glad you received my last, I certainly thought you would fail to get it on account of those detestable raiders.

Since I last wrote, again has the two opposing armies in Virginia, met in deadly strife. On the morning of the 30th July, the enemy sprung one of their mines in front of our lines, charging simultaneously with the explosion and succeeded in capturing a portion of our lines, held by Genl. Elliott's[4] S.C. brigade. About sunrise three brigades of our division, Mahonels[5], Wright's and Sanders', were ordered from the right of our lines to the point at which the explosion occured. Immediately upon their arrival, a charge was ordered, etc. Our brigade was ordered in before they were formed, thereby causing some little confusion. The works were

---

[4] Brigadier General Stephen Elliott, CSA
[5] Brigadier General William Mahone, CSA

carried & the enemy driven back to their old position. Upon the arrival of our troops at the breastworks, they were found to be filled with *real sure enough niggers* crying no quarter! no quarter!

As they were the first colored troops our troops had ever seen, you may rest assured "no quarter" was shown. An indiscriminate butchery commenced, and hardly a negro remained to tell the story. 'Twas awful to think of, but I suppose 'twas perfectly right. Not a single negro ought to have been captured.

Our loss was very heavy indeed. We have to mourn many dear friends, whose lives have been sacrificed to their country. Nearly every regimental commander was killed. Col. Evans, 64th Ga., Capt. Rush & Adjt. Levy, 22nd G, Capt. McCrea & Ensign Ryan 3rd Ga., were among the killed. The 64th Ga. lost 8 commissioned officers and a number of privates. The 3rd Ga. lost 18 killed on the field, two of the number from my company. Our company had, lst Lt. & four men *wounded*. The total loss in the brigade is two hundred and thirty one. That is a pretty heavy loss for a short engagement, isn't it? Most of our killed were decently buried in coffins. I believe the remains of some were sent to Georgia. Oh how many hearts have been made sad and desolate by that day's work. Just think of our brave men being murdered by cruel heartless negroes. Isn't it enough to render the Yankeys more despicable, if possible, than ever? Certainly a kind & just God will not permit such a people to rule over us. Oh how I do long for this cruel war to end & such barbarities with it.

There has been some uneasiness about home for fear the raiders would pay *them* a visit. The latest intelligence I've rec'd. reports their presence in our county; but as yet not our *town*. I know if they came to the *city* of Penfield Ma & Sis were nearly fightened to death. I am *almost afraid* to receive a letter from them. I try however and hope for the best. Others have fared much worse than they are likely to. The last letter I rec'd: stated that they were going to face them (the raiders) as best they could. I expect the people of S. Western Ga. are beginning to be somewhat alarmed also. I see that a raiding party had started in the direction of Macon & that Genl. Iverson, formerly of this army, had severly punished them, capturing the celebrated Stoneman of the Yankey army in this state. He will be remembered as having made a raid towards Richmond during the battle at Chancellorsville. I hope these raids will soon be made to cease by a complete defeat of Sherman. I don't think they will be able to capture any of our large troops, but they can nevertheless do a great deal of damage. I think we will hear of forest soon. If they visit *your* home give them a *plate of buttermilk and it will be all right.* You know Cavalrymen are peculiarly fond of that article. If I could see you, I could tell you some rich jokes. I can't write them so I will wait until I see you, which I hope will not be long.

Since I last wrote, one of our members[6] has been elected to a lieutenantcy in my company & this morning took command. In losing him as a mess mate, I've lost one of my best friends. We have messed together for the past three years hardly an unkind word passing between us. I do hope he may be spared from the enemy's bullets & be permitted to return safely home to enjoy a speedy and an honorable peace. I fully agree with you in the opinion that hostilities will cease before March. I have long since thought such would be the case. Since the 4th of May, our arms have been signally victorious. Almost everywhere except in Georgia, we've met with unprecedented success. It seems as if that department has been & is now our only drawback. I believe we would long since have had peace if that army could have equalled the successes of the "Army of Northern Virginia". I don't say this in a boast; I honestly believe it. In plain language, the misfortunes of that army have counterbalanced the successes of this. The ---- from that army continues to be the same, "little skirmishing & shelling along the lines". I hoped when Hood took command, Sherman would soon be compelled to leave Ga.; but from late accounts it seems he still hovers around Atlanta. If Joe Johnston had been in command, Atlanta would long since have been in possession of Sherman & company.

---

[6] Most likely Adrian S. Morgan

On the evening of the 4th inst., I had the good fortune to receive a box from Ga., filled with luxuries from home. You can easily imagine how much I appreciated and how thankful I was for it, when I tell you I've paid $3.00 dollars per quart for potatoes and $10.00 dollars per pound for butter, and everything else in proportion. I have become thoroughly disgusted with cornbread and blockade bacon. Recently we have drawn a little, very little, beef captured by Early in Pennsylvania. I am ashamed to say it; but I acted as if I had never seen anything to eat before. I couldn't help it, tho'. I expect if I should get home now and sit down to a well furnished table, I should render myself quite ridiculous. I hardly know how to use a knife and fork. Don't you *pity* me that I have backslided so? *Perhaps* after awhile, I will regain my *previously* attained *perfection in etiquette.* 'Tis to be hoped.

If the Yankeys have visited my home, I needn't look for another box soon; that's certain. I know everything they can lay their hands on, will be destroyed. Their previous conduct, warrants this prediction. I don't suppose the Yankeys in Georgia are more humane than those in Virginia. *Here*, they destroy not only destroy one's property; but the persons *themselves* are liable to insult and injury. The latest news we have is that Hood has been largely reinforced. If so, we anticipate good news soon. I only hope it may prove true.

You seem to be fearful that your relatives were in Pennsylvania with Early. They were not there in the first raid for I saw Jack during that time & I wrote you all about it; but I presume you haven't received my letter. Since that time, McLaw's Division has been sent to a point below Richmond. They may have gone elsewhere since that time, I can't say Early is again at work in the W. S., McLaw *maybe* with him. *We* have no means of knowing exactly the disposition of our troops. The people of Yaneydom seem to be somewhat enraged & frightened at the destruction of part of Chambersburg, Penn. I wonder if they ever think of how many *Southern* homes have been made desolate, by their ruthless raiders. They, when *their* homes are burned, are very quick to cry out against such warfare; proclaiming it barbarous and inhuman. They are a *wonderfully consistent* people. Everything *they* do is perfectly right. 'Tis to be devoutly wished they may soon meet their just rewards.

I have the honor to be the subscriber to the Illustrated News and hope it will greatly contribute to your enjoyment. I would have told you long since; but I was fearful you hadn't received it. I wish I could do more to make you happy. I know life at home now must be almost intolerable. You may hereafter receive it more regularly. I think the Novellette being published in it is quite interesting. I can't say however I recommend such literature.

I have seen one copy of the "Countryman" containing an account of race on Chicimocomico island, and think it is pretty correct. Although 'twas *old* to me, I was somewhat interested in it's recital. I am glad your interest is enlisted with the 3rd Ga. Aside from the motives that prompt you, I think you could not be interested in the welfare of a more patriotic body of men. I don't say it is the *best*; but 'tis as good as any. Its record will bear its already high reputation.

Genl. Wright's has for some time past been in Georgia on sick furlough. During his absence our brigade is commanded by V. J. B. Girardez[7] temporarily appointed Brig. Genl. He was formerly our Adjutant general, & has several times led the brigade into action. All seem very much pleased with the appointment and a great many desire it should be permanent. 'Tis reported that Genl. W. has been appointed Maj. Genl. of militia and will not return to this army. If so, Girardez will in all probability be our next Brigadier. Whoever is commander, I hope will be blessed with success, and sustain the well - --- character of all Georgia's soldiers. None nobler can the Confederacy claim. On *every* field they have proven themselves equal to the task imposed. This has been the point of honor.

Since commencing this letter I've been several times called off to cook (for I am chief in that department) and just now to get a letter from home, sweet home. I have just finished reading it and find all my fears about a raid into my *city* are wholly unfounded. All are well

---

[7] Brigadier General Victor J.B. Girardey, CSA

hopeful and not the least despondent. Pa says they will all soon be killed or captured. I hope so.

I hope you Father will continue to remain at home. I know he has done more for the Confederate Government than he could have by remaining in the *field*. Provisions are obliged to be raised, and I know of no one better calculated to superintend.

You say I complain of your short letters, and wish you could write long and interesting letters. You are mistaken, Mag, I only ask you to write me long letters, not that they are unacceptable or uninteresting. You *know* your letters are my chief source of pleasure. I wouldn't be debarred the privilege of receiving for anything in the world. I hope such may never happen. I think of you often and hope we will soon be happy together. Not a day passes but that my thoughts are of thee and thee only. Particularly is this the case since the two armies of Tennessee have beer transferred as it wer, to our rear doors. You know not to what agonizing suspense I'm subjected. I *hope*, however, for the best. Should the prospect for a peace look gloomy, don't for a moment think that I will prove false or unfaithful. I will ever through adversity & prosperity prove faithful to the vows I've made and I cannot believe but that you will act the same towards me. I know you will, Mag. I could not doubt, if I would. Excuse everything improper in this poor letter. I'm not at all in a *writing humor*. Love to all your Father's family & my friends. Write soon.

I remain as ever yours faithfully & devotedly,

Alva

Millwood, Georgia
19th Aug. 1864
Dear Alva,

Last mail brought me your most interesting letter of the 21st ultimo; and I respond by the earliest opportunity.

Cousin John G. came home last evening again surprising us very much. We were sitting in the front porch. I was reading by the light of a candle, it being about dark when he came walking up the steps before ever we discovered him. This was a complete and agreeable surprise to all. After supper, Pa and Ma went over home with him; there was great rejoicing. He is in bad health, has a sick furlough. The news from Virginia is quite cheering, Grant having been completely foiled in his last attempt to get Petersburg, has now gone in direction of Washington City, no doubt thinking he would capture Early's corps, but Genl. Lee happened to be smart enough for him, anticipated his design, and his Army or at least the greater portion of it is at Fredericksburg.

John parted with Brother at Fredericksburg depot. He was in excellent health and fine spirits. I do hope the campaign has closed for always. If he can escape the bullets from now till winter, I think very likely we will see him before a great while. I guess he feels almost alone now, his relatives all home. I am glad you visit him, and hope you will continue to do so, whenever you can. He is altogether ignorant of our present relations; but when I see him, I will enlighten him. Joe has his furlough extended 30 days longer. I am so glad they are both at home. I can but believe it a Providential occurrence coming at this time, while the family are in such deep distress. Sis has been quite sick, most of the time since her brother's death. She's improving now rapidly.

Since I commenced this letter, we have rec'd. some mail though no letters from Va. Our music we sent for some time ago has come. I will give you the names, "Lorena", "I Remember the Hour when sadly we parted", "Wait till the War Love is over" and "My Lone Rock by the Sea". I've heard most of them, and think them beautiful. The last mentioned, we sent for, in order to *get* double notes. I like it so much. "Her bright smile haunts me still" is a very sweet tune. I believe it is my favorite, though I have so many, it is a difficult matter to decide which I do like best.

We frequently play and sing "Lula is gone", it never fails to bring a remembrance of you.

I receive the "Southern Illustrated News" regularly now, a beautiful piece came out in the last number on Music, which was my sentiments exactly. Perhaps you have seen it, in July number 30th. "The hearts of Miriam Clyde" is also a good piece, in the same no.

What has become of Genl. Wright? I learn through the press that Capt. Girardez has been appointed to the temporary command of the brigade. I rather expect he has been promoted.

Genl. Hood still holds Atlanta, though a great many think, he will have to fall back. A regular engagement is daily looked for, at that point. Heavy fighting no doubt awaits us. If the enemy is successful what a sad fate to Georgia! I fear we will suffer from Yankee raids, so long as Sherman remains in the State.

I have not the slightest objection to the course you pursued relative to my letters. I had often thought I would ask you to destroy them,' knowing Soldiers had no way to preserve their letters at all times, but having neglected doing so; I'm perfectly satisfied with your disposal of them; tho they are such poor letters, I hated for any one to see them. I'm glad they made a favorable impression with your sister, and hope she may never have a cause to retract from her present opinion. of course, I love her too.

When you were to see us last, I had not a thought that you loved or thought of me otherwise than a friend. *I* had never thought or looked upon you only as a true friend, and not untill I received your declaration of love did I think that I loved you. I remember well the remark I made to you the day after your arrival, "that I had the day before seen my sweetheart, from Va., home on furlough." I had allusion to Mr. ---- you know whom I used to be teased about, living then near Henderson.

Whenever I see you, I will tell you more. You asked a lady when you were here last to select you a sweetheart, didn't you? I will simply say she has spoken many good words for you. She thinks a great deal of Old A. B. I expect this will be old when you rec'd it, as you have moved farther off. I shall continue to write often, and if you fail to receive my letters, don't attribute the delay to any neglect on my part. All send love.

Yours affectionately,

Mag

Petersburg, Virginia

August 28th '64

Dearest Maggie,

Again I'm indebted to you a letter, and I know not how I can better compensate you, than by an immediate reply. It seems from the terror (you expressed) that you have been misinformed as to the whereabouts of our army. You seem to have been, at the time of writing your last, fearful that I would fail to receive it "since we had moved farther off"; but I'm happy to say your fears were unfounded. I have derived great pleasure from the perusal of your letter and we are still ---- at the above named place. Since we've been compelled to remain here this long, I'm contented to remain until winter. True 'tis very disagreeable and monotonous; but considering the lateness of the season, I believe 'tis preferable to a *tour North*. Besides all this, I think the prospect for a *furlough* will much better here than on the march.

I am *truly* glad you've so far been spared the presence of the Yankey raiders; but from the recent dispatches of the press association, I'm every day afraid those uncivilized warriors will make their appearance near your home. It is doubtless their intention to free the prisoners confined at Andersonville. I hope such may never be. Should, however, such happen, I pity the fate of South Western Georgia. 'Twould be equivalent to turning loose so many inmates of the Asylum and Penitentiary. Neither citizens nor private property would be respected. Everything in their path would be taken or destroyed. Such has been the course pursued by them in Virginia, why should Georgia be an exception? I have known them to (take) jewelry from the persons of young ladies. Their object is to impoverish the citizens and enrich themselves. I do sincerely hope the day of retribution is not far distant. Sometimes I think *all* raiders ought to be put to death as soon as captured; but so soon as I see them, I pity and can but treat them as prisoners of war should be.

Since I last wrote, another signal victory has, by the blessing of God, been achieved by Confederate armies, I the battle was fought near Peanis Station about ten miles from this city on the railroad leading to Weldon. For a rarity our brigade was not engaged. Our loss is said to have been incredibly small. About twenty two hundred prisoners and nine pieces of artillery are the fruits of the victory to the Government. The troops engaged secured to themselves *many* little valuables.

They exchanged hats and shoes with each other, the consent of the "rebel" only being obtained. Almost every soldier is now provided with a Yankee watch. 'Tis surprising to see how much a soldier will expose himself to get a watch or something else of far less value. Some seem to fight for nothing but *plunder*. You would be surprised to see how many men in our army have tents, oil cloths, blankets, havresacks, canteens and many other articles of less value, all captured from the Grand Army of the Potomach.

I wrote you sometime since that Genl. Wright had gone home on sick furlough. I presume you've ere this received the letter to which I have allusion. I have recently heard from one source that he was transferred to the army around Atlanta, from another, that he was appointed to the command of the post at Augusta. So you see we do not *know exactly* "what has become of him"; *but* I think 'tis pretty certain he will never return to this *army*.

Capt. Girardez was appointed temporarily Brigadier General; but poor fellow, he was killed while gallantly disputing the advance of the enemy at New Market hill, below Richmond on the 16th ult. He was truly a brave and gallant soldier and greatly beloved by our whole brigade. His career although short, was bright and worthy of imitation by all. In his death our country lost one of its ablest defenders, Society one of its brightest ornaments.

I am again well and am fully able to eat all the Government gives me; but the fact of my being able to eat my rations is not of itself very strong proof of my recovery; for a very sick man could easily eat what we get & not feel any worse. We, however, get a sufficiency, such as it is. Corn bread and Nassau bread, sugar, and coffee have entirely "played out". I don't think there is any prospect of starvation if the Yankeys have got possession of the Weldon R.R. The South side road is still open. Since the occupation of the Weldon R.R., the supply of vegetables, in the markets, has been somewhat diminished. This is about the only injury inflicted. There is already enough provisions in Richmond to last the army twelve months or more. During the whole of last winter, provisions were carried to that city.

I am truly glad Jno. is at home, I know it must be a great comfort to his Mother and Sister to have John and Joe both home at the same time. I can heartily sympathize with John in his sickness. I think whenever a person is too sick to perform military duty, he ought to be sent home, he can recover sooner and be of less expense to the Government. Of course, I've no objection to your telling Jack of our engagement. If I thought it proper, I would do it myself. I *prefer*, however, that *you* should acquaint him with the facts.

I have sometimes thought that I would write to your Father and procure his sanction; but after mature reflection I have concluded that it is best to approach him in person. What do you think of it? I shall be guided wholly by *your* decision. I can do either.

You speak of several pieces that have recently appeared in the "Illustrated News". I am glad you receive it regularly. I haven't seen a copy since we left winter quarters. From some cause, none are brought to the army to sell. Has the "Rivals" been finished? How did you like it? From reading the first number I predicted that story would be quite interesting. Although I don't approve of novel reading to excess, I, sometimes indulge, especially while in camp. Reading matter, now, is very scarce. The daily papers are read from beginning to end, the advertisements inclusive.

I have heard most of the pieces of music you enumerated, and think them all very pretty. Being a lover of music of any kind, I can hardly tell you which I think prettiest. I think, however, "My love Rock by the Sea" and "Her bright smiles haunt me still" are my favorites. The latter especially; for truly Mag, your "bright smiles haunt me still". I think of you often, and hope, oh how sincerely, I may soon see you.

From the tone of the Yankey press, I think Peace is speedily and surely coming. Everything indicates it, and I can but believe that this "cruel war" will end by March '65. I am looking forward to the meeting of the Convention with *breathless* anxiety; for 'tis *there* we are to look for the first introductory step toward peace. If a peace democrat is nominated, I believe he will be elected, and there will follow a recognition of the Confederacy, and peace and happiness will soon hover over our now distracted country.

Millwood, Georgia
Sept. lst 1864
Dearest Alva,
A few days since I had the happy pleasure of perusing another of your most welcome letters, dated 21st ultimo.

Last evening we rec'd mail. I see we have achieved a great victory on the Weldon railroad. Gen. Hill made the attack and at the second assault, he carried their entire line of work. The loss of the enemy reported heavy, ours relatively small. I had hoped the campaign in Virginia had closed, but no such good luck yet. I'm truly glad the 18th Ga. left before the fight came off. We haven't heard from Jack in some time, though presume he is some where near Culpepper.

I have been thinking A. P. Hill's corps. had gone in the direction of the valley; but have been under a wrong impression, so I learn.

Sherman has abandoned his entrenchments on his left and centre, and is massing on the left of Hood, with a view not fully explained. He is either playing a trick to deceive Hood, or his retreat has commenced.

Reports say Genl. Wheeler is doing much damage to the enemy, and that Sherman's communications have been effectively cut. I hope his whole army will soon be driven out of this state. We are very tired of his long visit, indeed we should have thanked him not to have come at all.

Yesterday I was over to see Miss Amelia, who was at Macon visiting her relatives when the Raiders attacked that place. I was much amused hearing her tell how she cried and wished herself in Dooly.

She has recently rec'd a letter from a cousin of hers, Newman Pounds, as he is a member of your Regt. and is now at home on furlough. He wrote "She must come to see him, he would tell her something about Mr. Spencer; he had heard him speak of her".

She doesn't like this cousin of hers at all and said she didn't expect to go to see him; though couldn't imagine what he had to tell her about you. She doesn't know that you and I even correspond, I told her she ought to go to see him. I would like to hear the message, she will tell me I know if she hears it. Then I'll tell you, wouldn't you like to hear it?

Samantha has come in here (parlor) and is now playing the piece you sent us, "Rock beside the Sea". I wish you could hear it, tis beautiful. Samantha is perfectly delighted with it.

When you come to see us we will be prepared to give you some good music as we are practicing a good many new pieces. If you could happen in some evening between sun set and dark, you would think us particular fond of music, as we practice at that hour most every day.

John & Joe are flying around enjoying themselves finely. One night this week they serenaded us. Joe performs better on the violin than he used to and is the greatest mimic I ever saw. If you visit his co. again and he is present, make him sing for you. Pa has promised to give them a dinner before they return back, and invite all the girls, and the fine boys that are left; or are at home. Though I don't know for certain he will. I will give you an invitation if it comes off.

Yesterday evening a Capt. of the 4th Ga. called to see us. I heard in the morning that it was very probable he would call in the evening, and we went off visiting on purpose. He was to see John & Joe in forepart of the day. We don't like him much, of course, or we shouldn't left home. I would write oftener, but have only one day in each week that we can send off letters. Sometimes when I have the time, to write company prevents. I have to delay another week. Though, rest assured I will write as often as I can. Write again soon, your letters serve to while away many lonely hours. They are my chief source of pleasure. I hope to see you soon. I shall send this letter to Perry to mail as I have an opportunity.

Cross Writing:
This leaves all well, in the possession of fine spirits and the expectation of a pleasant time.

I hope this may find you the same. All send love. As ever yours devotedly, Maggie

Petersburg, Virginia
September 16th 1864
Dearest Maggie,
After a delay of two weeks, your most interesting letter, of the lst ult., was received yesterday. Isn't it too bad to be compelled to wait so long before hearing from those we love? I have delayed writing sometime hoping to hear from you; but I was so often disappointed, yours of yesterday was quite a surprise. I was so sadly disappointed I even commenced a letter to you; but after reflection I concluded to wait a little while longer, and tore up what I had written. Knowing that Andersonville was *the* point which Sherman was so anxious to

possess, and knowing too that you were not very far distant, I was every day fearful that the raiders had made their appearance.

Since your last was ritten Atlanta has fallen. What has been the effect produced upon the people of Georgia, I can't tell; but I'm afraid the people have become somewhat discouraged, I hope not though.

Its capture, did at first, I'm sorry to say, have quite a demorallizing effect on our army; but since the true condition of affairs has been made known, the same determined resistance and hatred to the Yankeys has returned stronger, if possible, than ever.

As to the cause of our failures in Georgia, of course, I'm not able to judge, but from all I can learn I'm fully convinced that your opinion, of the incompetency of Hood to command so large an army was correct. I judged his ability by his previous successes while in command of a division in *this* army. It does really seem that nothing but reverses can be looked for from our armies in Ga. I hope however and believe that ere long the deeds of that army will eclipse any thing that has been by the Army of Northern Virginia. You may think from the above, that I'm proud to belong to Genl. Lee's army. Well, I am, and I believe 'tis an honor too. Ought I not to feel so?

Everything now indicates that a heavy engagement is every day expected. A day or two since ---- advanced on his left (our right), with the intention no doubt of cutting the South Side R.R. A great many troops have been sent from our left and went to meet him. Yesterday evening a good large number of troops passed through Petersburg. I've heard since that 'twas Kershaw's[8] division returned from the valley. If Wofford's[9] brigade is any where near us, I will use every effort in my power to see Jack. Since their division left this place, the above brigade has been engaged with the enemy, and *report* says, they suffered considerably how true I can not tell. I think there can be but little doubt about their being near this place. From all I can learn, the lines of these two armies confront each other running

---

[8] Brigadier General Joseph Brevard Kershaw, CSA
[9] Brigadier General William Tatum Wofford, CSA

east and west, before north and south. Evidently some grand movement is progressing.

---- out everything about me that Newman could tell. I know she will think me a strange being to be talking about one with whom I had spent so short a time. I can't imagine what Newman desires to tell him about *me*; for I have never said but very little to him about Miss P. merely inquired when he had heard from her, and remarked that I thought she was a *very* nice young lady. I wish I could say I entertaines as high an opinion of him as I do of her. He doesn't belong to the 3rd Ga. now, he has been transferred to the 64th Ga. of our brigade. He was wounded in one of the battles around this city. I hope Miss M. will go to see him, she may be able to cheer his *drooping spirits* and *give him some advive*. My respects to her & tell her *not to believe anything he says about me unless it be good*, for *you* know I'm a *"mighty good boy"*.

I am glad you both are so well pleased with the music I sent you. I hope soon to hear you play it. You know I'm exceedingly fond of music. I think of goint to see some of the Petersburg ladies this week, if nothing prevents, just to get them to play and sing for me. I'll try and not be captivated. I thank you for your invitation to dinner. If I'm not there, *think of me*.

Another birthday 6th of Sept., has rolled 'round, and still this cruel war is raging. That day was remarkably quiet and beautiful; nothing transpiring to distinguish it from other days. I didn't even have anything good to eat. A few days after, though I received a box from home, having besides other luxuries a large *"birth day cake"*. You may be sure I enjoyed it considerably. I hope I may spend my next in Georgia in peace and happiness.

I'm glad the Ga. Militia have been permitted to visit their homes even for a short time. I only wish I could receive a furlough for the same length of time, I think I could enjoy myself finely.

Winter is fast making its appearance, and in it I can see nothing but hardship, danger and suffering. Owing to the scarcety of wood, we can but fear suffering from cold, if nothing else. I believe if any one can bear it I can. I will try (I can't do otherwise). It is evidently the intention of both armies to winter around this place unless the movements now in progress materially change affairs.

I hope ere long we may meet each other to rejoice over a peaceful, prosperous and happy country. Although our letters sometimes fail to reach their destination, write often. Though we are separated far from each other, I will remain your true and devoted,

Alva

Love to all.

Petersburg, Virginia
September 24th 1864
Dearest Maggie,

This is a dull, rainy and dreary day well calculated to make one feel deeply, darkly, desperately blue, and I know not how I can better drive away my ennui than by writing to *you*. I confess however that in my present situation, I'm not at all fit to interest anyone and I am *almost* inclined to shrink from all risk. I didn't mean to say that, Mag; if you will permit, I'll retract and say, "I'm almost inclined to shrink from exposing my *inability*; for I assure you 'tis no task to write to you, 'tis indeed a pleasure surpassed by no other, except the perusal of your dear letters. If it were possible I could wish I might receive them every day.

I expect you would now like to know the *cause* of my being so "desperately blue". Well I will commence by telling you I formed some very pleasant lady acquaintance last night in the city of Petersburg. They were very pretty indeed, their names Lou and Joe - ---. I'm afraid that, if my entire thoughts had not been upon a certain Maggie, I would have come away minus a heart. Methinks I see you frowning. You mustn't get mad now, for you know "*native* will out". I know only one way by which you can make me refrain and that is take me away from Petersburg and out of the army. Besides their being so fascinating and such brilliant conversationists, they were excellent performers on the piano. They sang at my special request "My lone rock by the sea". It was the first time I had ever heard it sung by two ladies and I thought it beautiful. 'Twas my first visit; but if we remain near Petersburg, I don't intend it shall be my *last*. Do you blame me to enjoy myself if I can? I know you do not. That is the only innocent amusement we have and seldom that, unless we are stationed near a city.

Yesterday (negro like), I got a pass and walked down into Petersburg to see what damage had been done to the buildings by the shells of the enemy. The damage done can be easily repaired in one month, the newspaper accounts to the contrary, notwithstanding. You would be surprised to see the stores on Sycamore street, the most exposed and principal one in the city. They are full, to overflowing with goods, of every description. True, a great many dwelling houses have been deserted, still a great many are now occupied. I confess the people of Petersburg, especially the ladies, are braver than I would be for I'm certain I wouldn't live in a house exposed to the shells fo the enemy, no longer than was necessary for me to move away. Every thing seems to move on just as if they were in perfect security. I suppose the people are becoming used to it by this time. They have become reckless.

The two armies around this city still occupy their old relative position; but the situation tomorrow may be quite different. I'm looking every day to hear that Grant is moving to the right to cut off our communication by the South side railroad. When that movement commences, there will be hard fighting. I only hope our brigade will be permitted to occupy its present position on the lines. The same incessant piquet firing and canonading is kept up day and night. Almost every day I see some poor fellow brought out a corpse or badly wounded. As yet, the piquet lines in front of our brigade are peaceable; but we are looking every day for to them to commence sharpshooting in *our* front too.

From all accounts, our forces under Genl. Earley have met with a serious defeat. As I see no account of any other forces being engaged except Rode's[10] and Breckenridge's[11] divisions, I presume Kershaw's was not engaged. Again we have to mourn the loss of another of our most efficient officers. He was surely beloved by his entire division and his loss will be deeply felt. I *hope* no further loss will befall us there. I think Earley will be able to hold his present position against a very large force of the enemy. A great many suppose that Sheridan[12] has received heavy reinforcements from Sherman. I am myself inclined to that opinion too. Our cause is now at a point more critical than ever before known. If we can but be successful for *one year* longer, I think all danger will have passed.

Sherman still occupies Atlanta and I'm afraid he will soon pay his respects to other portions of our beloved state. I'm afraid his visit will be rather longer than you expected. He is daily running six or eight raids loaded with commissary and smaller stores, into the city preparatory, I've no doubt, to sending the greater portion of his army elsewhere. I don't generally make prophecies; but I'm going to make one now. I predict that in less time than six months, Genl. Hood's army will be feasting on the Yankee rations now in Atlanta. All Sherman's boastings will be but to his shame. He will surely meet with his just deserts for the manner in which he treated the people of that afflicted city. I hope ere this all those who desired have been removed into our lines, where they will receive that protection due them.

I received a letter from Sister yesterday, saying they were still living in dread of Yankee raiders. I do hope her fears may prove groundless; but I'm afraid 'twill be a forlorn hope. I think it is Sherman's intention to inflict as great injury upon the people of Ga. as he possibly can. 0 how I do pity those who are so unfortunate as to be in their line of march. May *you* and others, dear to me, escape that dreadful calamity.

---

[10] Major General Robert Emmett Rhodes, CSA
[11] General John Cabell Breckinridge, CSA
[12] Major General Philip Henry Sheridan, USA

Has Miss Pounds been to see Newman? If so, you must tell me what he was so anxious to "tell her about Mr. Spencer". I thought *then*, as I do *now*, that was a mere *ruse* to induce her to visit him. It was merely one of his *strategic movements*.

How is Miss Sis? You haven't mentioned anything about her in so long that I'm afraid she's become teased or offended at something I've written. If so, tell her to forgive me and let's make friends. I suppose ere this Jno. and Joe have returned to Virginia. I had thought that probably they would come through this city and I would see them; but as they are in the valley now, I presume they will go direct to Richmond. I should like very much indeed to see them.

I expect after reading this and seeing what an effect last night's frolick has produced, you will advise me to refrain in the future, I hope *not* though, for I think I will become more used to it after awhile. You know any sudden change produces *physical* derangement, why not mental? The pleasure was too great and sudden. If the meeting of strange ladies produced so much pleasure, how is it possible for me to estimate that I would experience in *your* presence? I really do believe I would render myself ridiculous. To prevent any such contingency, I will continue to visit the young ladies of Petersburg, and by the time I *get a furlough*, I will be better prepared to meet you.

I have just said above that "I hoped I would be better prepared by the time I got a furlough", which I do sincerely hope will not be long. You know not, Mag, how extremely anxious I am to see you and tell you how unbounded and unmeasurable is my love for *you*. I have often told you in my feeble letters that I love you more than all earth, besides; but I think if you— "Could look into my heart, And see your image there, You would see the sunny loveliness, Affection makes it wear".

You would be better satisfied of the truth of my declaration from one look into my *face*, than from all that I've written since I first told you of my love. I know Mag, that you are confident I love you; but I wish to make *you* as confident of *my* love as I am of *yours*. Almost every day, every hour, I long to be permitted to see you soon.

I know you will become tired reading this long uninteresting letter; but I hope you excuse me this time, for I feel like I could sit and write to you all day long. Each scratch of the pen seems to transport me to your side, and I assure you that would be the happiest moment of my life. While I am writing to *you*, I think of *you*, and none of the daily scenes of camp life trouble me in the least. I believe if I had nothing else to do but to write I would get along very well. Do you wonder at my sometimes being a little melancholly? I think I am perfectly excusable. I am naturally of a buoyant disposition; but I confess I am very often low spirited to say the least of it.

Our cause now looks gloomy. Our armies are suffering defeats, and every thing looks anything but peaceful. Our many enemies are putting forth every energy to crush and annihilate the rebels. Although this dark cloud of oppression is hanging over our beloved land, threatening to spend its fury upon us, still I believe it has a "silver lining" and will soon pass away, revealing to us a happy and prosperous country. There is an old saying that "the darkest hour is just before day", doesn't it seem as if it were nearly day? I think our cause is more dark and disperate to-day than it has ever been. If it becomes much worse, we will surely suffer. I firmly believe tho' that a just God will not permit our cruel enemies to rule over us. He has promised to protect us, and I believe he will surely do it. Let us all --- ourselves for the coming conflict, and prepare to meet it with calmness and resignation. After that is passed we will enjoy an honorable peace and be a free and happy people.

We continue to receive plenty to eat & plenty to wear, I mean a sufficiency. I heard one of my comrades say the other day that the commissary had figured a calculated ---- enough that they had found out exactly the quantity of flour and meat necessary to keep a man in good working order, and that was all they issued us. I believe it too; for we don't have a particle to throw away. Not long since Genl. Wade Hampton with his cavalry succeeded in capturing from the enemy near City point, 2,500 fine beeves, plenty enough to subsist our army 10 or 15 days. 'Twas quite a dangerous expedition, having to go almost entirely around Grant's army. The Yankeys are very chagrined at their ineffectual attempt to recapture the property lost. They acknowledge it to have been a brilliant exploit. Don't you suppose Hampton's boys felt very proud, driving so many cattle into our lines? They certainly deserve great credit, both officers and men. Besides the cattle, they also captured three or four hundred prisoners and several pieces of artillery.

Every thing was brought safely into our lines, except for ----. ---- the cavalry in our army has been considered inferior to that of the western army, but if Forrest and Wheeler[13] will only do as much to harrass Sherman, I think Atlanta will soon be free from Yankey rule. Surely they have ample room for a display of their military genius. I hope they *may* succeed yet. If they do not do something and that very soon, they will not come up to the expectations of their friends.

I am afraid you cannot read this after I've written it. If you do suffer any difficulty, tell me and I will refrain in the future. You know why I write crossways, of course, I'll not be offended if you prefer it otherwise. I hope to receive a letter from you today. I look every mail until it does come. Write often Mag, you know not how much pleasure it affords me to hear from you. My love to all your Father's family, Miss Sis and all my friends. With a fond hope of hearing from you soon, I remain yours affectionately and devotedly,

Alva

PS. I have just received yours of the 16th and you know not with what pleasure I perused its contents. I am truly glad to know that Jack was safe when last heard from so hope he may continue to be so fortunate. I admire your opinion in reference to a reconstruction of the union, they are my sentiments exactly. I hope your remarks ---- as predictions will come true, but I hardly think we will have ---- so short a time and have enough ---- for the capture of Atlanta ---- have

---

[13] Lieutenant General Joseph Wheeler, CSA.

been so completely fooled by Sherman. I do so much wish I could be with you now, and if I couldn't be of assistance to you by making syrup, I could certainly enjoy eating it. Never mind, maybe I'll get to eat some of it yet. *You must save me some.* I recollect now who gave me the name of "Old AB". My respects. I am perfectly willing to ---- it until I see your Father before I attempt to get *hers* somehow. I hope too that will not be long ----. I will write again soon.

Affectionately,
Alva

Since the removal of Genl. Wright, I doubt that I direct my letters right. If not, you must tell me how. Mag.

Millwood, Georgia

October 3rd 1864

Dearest Alva,

Day before yesterday I rec'd your most welcome letter of the 16th ultimo. Its long delay caused *me* to be several times sadly disappointed and I know of no way to remedy the evil, only for us to write often and I will endeavor in the future to do so as often as I can, and I believe you will do the same, won't you?

The reception of your letter relieved our minds of considerable fear relative to the whereabouts of Brother. We were fearful he was in those recent engagements in the Valley, indeed had no other thought till I received your letter. You know not how glad we were that our conjectures were wrong. Our army correspondent "P.W.A." says in his letter to the Savannah Republican Henshaw's Division was not in the battle, having been sent off on detached service a few days before. I hope they may not be sent back to the Valley any more. It grieves me much to hear of our defeats there, coming just after our reverses here in this state. I believe the people have fully recovered now from the discouraging effects produced by the fall of Atlanta. I don't hear any advocate reconstruction. All seem to be, since seeing Genl. Hood's communication to Sherman, and hearing President

Davis' speech in Macon on his visit to Genl. Hood's headquarters, more determined than ever if possible, not to be subjugated.

Have you seen Hood's and Sherman's letters relative to the removal of the citizens out of Atlanta? If I knew you hadn't, I would send them to you, they are interesting. I cut them out of a paper last week and sent them in a letter to Brother. He frequently complains of not having anything to read during leisure hours. We very often send him some little reading matter that we think will interest him.

I'm unable to enlighten you with any new incidents from our army, or allow me, to call it, merely the Georgia army. I don't like to claim it ours so long as it meets with so many reverses.

The usual phrase may be added, "All is quiet along the line". So far as we know, and of their exact position, we are equally ignorant.

My greatest fear is now, of Grant's cutting off our communications with Virginia. If he should in his attempt be successful in taking the South Side R.R., I know I shall be very unhappy. Life then would surely be almost intolerable. But I will *hope* for the better. You say "You are proud to belong to Genl. Lee's army". I've heard the same expression from many who belonged to that army and I agree with you that you ought to consider it an honor.

In my last, I think I said it was thought Genl. Bragg[14] would supercede Hood, it should have been Beauregard, though he hasn't done so yet, but many think it probable. I see the leading officers have not lost confidence in Hood yet.

I would tell you that Captain's name whom I spoke of in my previous letter, but I entertain such a poor opinion of him, I don't even want to write his name in a letter of mine. He is of the 45th Geo., not the 48th and is now discharged from service. You know there are many officers who are not worthy the position they occupy.

---

[14] General Braxton Bragg, CSA

Millwood, Georgia
October 14th 1864
Dearest Alva,

Your most interesting and lengthy letter of the 24th ult was received a few days since. Twas my intention to have written several days previous to now; but I haven't been well. I feel better today than I have in a week. There is much sickness in our neighborhood. Sis Graham has been very sick. I sit up there last night to assist in giving physic. She was much better this morning and I think will be well in a few days.

Pa is complaining today. I hope tis nothing more than cold. Such a sudden change in the weather is I guess what has produced so much sickness. It has been very cold for the past week. Several mornings had white frost. Farmers are busy gathering their crops. The corn crop is not so good this year as last. The potato and cane crops are very good. In a short time we will commence making syrup and sugar from the "good cane" as the children call it. We will certainly have some for you when you come to see us.

Mail was brought out yesterday and I had hoped to get another letter but was disappointed. I expect you have called on those young ladies again in Petersburg and has produced such an effect as to render you totally unable to compose your mind long enough to write a letter. Now if you don't mind you will arouse a little jealous spirit. You say you know only one way by which I can make you refrain and that is "take you away from Petersburg and out of the army". Is it in my power to do that? I'm certainly at a loss to know what course to pursue. They have the advantage while I can only hear from you, they can see you, but I will content, I have the oldest claim.

I haven't the slightest objection of your visiting them once and awhile, but you must bear in mind, "Short and seldom visits make long friends".

There is a very nice Government agent calls here occasionally' in passing, whom I'm often teased about; but for what reason I don't know for I have never spoken half a dozen words to him, and is never in his company only at the table but I believe it is customary for young ladies to be teased about every young gentleman that calls. So if you fall in love with those Petersburg ladies, I don't know but that I'll "set my cap". But now laying all jests aside, Alva I never have a doubt but you'll prove true to all you have ever said.

When you first addressed me I confess I couldn't help but have some doubts; but in a short time you removed entirely all. I know you better now and the more I learn, the more I love.

Last winter when your furlough was disapproved you said you thought when you made application again you wouldn't say anything about it, to prevent anyone from being disappointed. Now, I do think you ought to tell me. Very often I leave home to spend a few days with my relatives and friends and when you come I want to be at home. It would certainly be a sad disapointment were you to come and I be from home. So it is a special request of mine that you must tell me.

When I last wrote I thought Kenshaw's division was at or near Petersburg, but since then a member of Jack's Co. has come home on furlough. A few days before the fight in the valley this division was ordered to Petersburg when they arrived at Culpepper, remained there only long enough to rest and was ordered back reeinforce Easily.

Jack wrote while at Culpepper, but when this member of his Co. left they were at Staunton and Jack was unwell. We will not be surprised any day to see him home as he is next

P.S. Excuse red ink, tis the best I can do.

Maggie

Petersburg, Virginia
October 15th 1864
Dearest Maggie,

Yesterday I was again rejoiced at the reception of another of your most interesting letters, and I hasten to reply, for fear we may both again be "sadly disappointed" by the long delay of our letters. I need not tell you how happy I was made by its perusal, you *know nothing* could have rendered me *more* happy. I heartily approve of your proposition to writ *often*, *you* know I write as often as possible, and *I* am as equally confident that *you* will do the same. Nothing could afford me greater pleasure than a *frequent* reception of your dear letters. You needn't fear that their frequent visits will detract from their value, I assure you, however often they come, my delight will not be lessened, but increased; and I will continue, as now, to prize them more highly, than any memento I possess.

I am very glad indeed that the reception of my last, dispersed the uneasiness you felt concerning your Brother, and I wish I could again tell you something about him; but I'm as wholly unable to give you any information concerning the movements of the army in the Valley, as the most ignorant slave. Everything connected with that and the army in our own lovely state, seems to be enveloped in mystery, which none, save those in their emmediate fields of operation, need attempt to unravel. I can very easily understand, the cause of the scarcity of news from Ga. It is, no doubt, witheld to prevent the authorities in Washington from gaining any information in reference to the army around Atlanta and not that the news is of such a character as to warrant its being held from the people. I have too much confidence in our authorities, for a moment to believe they would withhold from the people *anything*, good or bad.

You know not how glad I am to know that the people of Georgia have again determined *never* to be subjugated. I confess I, at one time, feared that, those *few* excerable reconstructionists, would cause some trouble in our already deeply afflicted country; but thanks to a brave and patriotic people, such sentiments have been crushed, and the "Empire State of the South" is as uncompromising as ever. Aside from the many other Sacrafices our noble people have made, isn't the fact, that amidst the darkest hour of our history, our people have again expressed their determination to be free, enough to cause every Georgian's heart to leap for joy? Such a people can *never* be conquered. Pres. Davis' recent visit to Ga., has, I've no doubt, had an influence in producing this glorious change among our people; but I think, by far the greatest influence has been excited by the ladies discountenancing the laggards and skulkers. Always, when dark clouds of oppression were lowering over our devoted country, threatening to engulph us in everlasting disgrace and infamy, they, the "Women of the South", were seen alleviating the sufferings of the sick and wounded soldiers, encouraging the despondent, and frowning upon the inactive, and exerting themselves to their utmost, in securing the liberties of their country. Shall such labors go unrewarded? No- You will surely receive the thanks of a grateful people, and the smiles and adulations of a gallant Southern soldiery. "Exert then your influence, ye virtuous fair- that influence with which the God of Nature has richly endowed you! Employ all the persuasive eloquence of chaste affection, in ceaseless efforts to diminish the sum of human guilt and misery; so will you prove yourselves Angels of mercy, sent in compassion to man to sooth his sorrows and alleviate his accumulated sufferings?"

My requesting you to present my respects to a lady, with whom I was only partially acquainted, and who knew nothing of our corre- spondence even, was surely an act of inexcusable thoughtlessness; but *you* will excuse me this time, won't you?

You, of course, are to determine who shall be your "confident". That Miss *Sis* should know of our relations, I haven't the least objection. I always respected her highly, and placed the utmost confidence in the pureness of her friendship, and during my stay in Dooly, I formed no more pleasant an acquaintance. Many thanks to her for her kind solicitude in my welfare, and remember me to her as *ever*, her most sincere friend. May Heaven's choicest blessings attend her, and may she obtain every desire.

Who could have given you such a favorable description of her, I so dearly love, I can't imagine. It must surely have been one with whom I'm personally and intimately acquainted. Ever since the reception of your letter, I've tried my best to guess; but you say *your* friend was told this a "*little* more than two years ago", and I know not a single acquaintance of mine, who was in Dooly or Houston, at that time. At first I thought 'twas a Miss Mason, who taught music in Haynesville before the war, and that she told Miss Poole. I next thought 'twas Dr. Everett. If 'tis not *one* of these, I give it up. Since I've tried so hard to guess, I don't think you ought to keep me in suspense any longer. I would indeed like to know of any one who entertained such an exalted opinion of my Mother. You must tell me next time. I do wish I could get some joke on you, I would make *you* guess some too. Never mind, when I see Joe, I will find out some joke on you!

I hardly know to what brigade I do belong. We've had so many commanders, I don't know who claims us. Continue tho', to direct as before. I don't think I've ever failed to receive any of your letters. 'Tis said that Genl. Sorrell[15] (formerly Longstreet's Adjt. Genl. & recently promoted to Brig. Genl.) will soon take command of our brigade. I don't know whether I will like the change or not.

I think, Mag, you needn't feel any uneasiness in reference to Grant's capturing the South side R.R. Our officers are all equal to the emergency. Our troops are in better spirits than I ever saw in my life. All seem confident that this is the last year of the war.

I wrote to you the other day; but since you say we must write oftener I've written again. Write often, Mag, whether you receive my letters or not, I will do the same.

I continue to hope we may see each other soon. You know not with what pleasurable emotions I anticipate it. I hope I will not be

---

[15] Brigadier General G. Moxley Sorrell, CSA

disappointed. I will say again, *write often*. My love to all your Father's family & all *enquiring* friends. Ever yours devotedly,

Alva

Middle Town, Va.
Oct. 20th 1864
My Dear Father,
Knowing your anxiety to know my fate, I embrace this opportunity for the purpose of sending you a short note. I was captured in the action of yesterday and am doing well. J. T. Hanard, J. A. Lockerman, T. R. Bullington and T. S. Lasseter are with me, all well. Henry Angley of Dooly is also here, and well.

You need not suffer any uneasiness about me. I will write every opportunity.

Give my love to all and reserve a goodly portion for yourself. As ever your affectionate son til death.

Andrew J. Cone

(A. J. (Jack) Cone – 18th Georgia, Co I, Brother of Margaret L. Cone)

Millwood, Georgia
October 25th 1864
Dearest Alva,
Today I have been made the recipient of your last most interesting letter of the 15th inst., also three or four days previous of one bearing date the 10th inst. They were gladly received and perused with *great* pleasure. I know it is the long delay of *my* letters that causes us to fail to receive our letters at the expected time and I will try to explain to you why this has been the case. Our facilities here for obtaining or sending off mail are very poor, only have a weekly mail, unless Pa or Mr. Henry happens to have business that calls them to Vienna between mail days, then they bring it out. So you see when we receive a letter it matters not how anxious we are to

reply, have to wait a whole week before we can have any opportunity to mail a letter, unless by mere chance we can send elsewhere and that is very seldom. The only way for me to remedy the delay is to write every week, and I don't really see how I can do that all the time. I most always do my writing on Friday, the day before we receive mail, and it is frequently the case company comes in and prevents, at other times, I'm so busily engaged at work, I'm compelled to postpone till the next or mail, but I will make this promise to write every week when I can or as often as I possibly can. I know you do not ask more. I'm glad at any time to hear from you and am confident you will not delay longer than you can avoid. Nothing affords me greater pleasure than a perusal of your letters. I hope the time is not far distant when we shall see each other. I do really think you ought to be permitted to visit Georgia this winter. Two years is a long time to be kept from home enduring so many hardships, sufferings and dangers.

We are very uneasy about Brother as he was sick when last heard from and had been for two weeks. Though he was with his company but unable for duty. It has been three years since he came home. He is pretty certain of a furlough soon. We are all *so* anxious to see him, I *do* hope we will see him very soon.

John and Joe are yet at home. They have stayed a good long time. I think it is their intentions to start back to their command next week.

I hardly think Joe can tell you any jokes on me; but on the contrary, I could tell some rich ones on him. He is quite a tease, and would doubtless like to tell you something that he thought you could tease me about; but he would have to make it, I know if he tells anything. He is a good boy, and is loved by all. We all will be quite lonely when they leave.

And you can't imagine who gave such a favorable description of your Mother. I will simply say you are personally and intimately acquainted with the person, and may be a member of your Co. now, as he used to be. Now guess again. I haven't a word of news to write concerning the two armies, in this state. Hood, though, is certainly in Sherman's rear, and doing much damage.

Tomorrow all the militia have been ordered to report to Genl. Smith, otherwise they will be treated as deserters. Several of our neighbors leave early in the morning. Some of whom I expect to send the letter by to mail.

I enclose a speech of Herchel V. Johnson's, or rather a letter. I like it very much. Pa says it is his sentiment exactly. Please excuse a half sheet. I write so in order to send the speech. Babe is quite sick of chills & fever. The family otherwise is in good health. Sis G. is well and sends her best respects, also Aunt Nancy and family. With a hope of seeing you soon, I remain as ever, yours devotedly, Mag

Petersburg, Virginia
November 6th 1864
Dearest Maggie,
"Alas! how light a cause may move
Dissensions between hearts that love".

Just think how indiscreet we have acted toward each other in our last letters to each other. *I* imprudently uttering thoughts of which I was heartily ashamed before they had even been sealed, and *you* in the most mild and pleasant tone cautioning me to refrain "lest such a course should cause dissension between hearts that loved". Oh why was I at that moment, *so* unguarded as to utter that which I've since, *so much* regretted, and which has caused *you*, for a moment, to fear or doubt. I think tho' I've in penitence, dearly paid for that unthoughtedness. But I must say *that* episode in our hitherto pleasant intercourse (the course of true love never did run smooth, to the contrary), has exhibited in your character traits that make you dearer, if possible, than ever. I've seen that you are sensibly alive to *anything* that looks like an estrangement, and are ready to rebuke any recurring waywardness or thoughtlessness. I indeed thank you from my heart for such a timely warning and such an affectionate check to

my innocently hazardous conduct; and as though our love has been
disturbed and the once peaceful tranquility marred-

"Dearer seems each dawning smile
For having lost its light while"
And although I *know* you've been *offended*
"The short passing anger but seemed to awaken
New beauty like flowers that are sweetest when shaken".

It has often been said that long engagements are dangerous, that
they are seldom consumated. They are at least objectionable (in times
of peace), but let us each endeavor to prove this adage entirely false
and unfounded. With Divine assistance it shall *never* be confirmed by
my conduct. Believe me when I tell you, that when this cruel war shall
have ceased, you'll find that the pure love and fond devotion I *now*
cherish for *you* has not been disregarded and estranged; but has been
nourished and strengthened amid the most trying temptations and
excruciating hardships, and I doubt not your pure heart will cordially
reciprocate.

If I have heretofore *written*, or should in the future, *write* such
things as are calculated to give offence, be assured, 'tis because I've
never kept anything from you; but have always opened my heart to
you; that you might see *there* how deeply your image is engraven
upon its most sacred tablets. You've been so kind to me. Whenever
you have doubted you've told me so, and whenever there has been
the slightest differences, I could not, had I been disposed, attach any
blame or want of sincerity to *you;* but have *always* found that *I* had
erred and not *you*. It has always been my most heartfelt desire and
most devout wish to prove to you my unchangeable love and
devotion, and if at any time I've appeared unnecessarily importunate,
'twas not because I thought you didn't appreciate and reciprocate the
truth and warmth of my attachment; but because I thought you *didn't*
express all you felt.for me. My heart did indeed leap with joy when
you told me "the heart I give you *can not* love more fond and true",

and implied more, and our hearts were *that day* forever indissolubly linked together' but oh had we expressed ourselves more fully to each other, how far less liable, would we have been to disturbances from trivial causes.

Since I last wrote, quite an interesting scene has been enacted in front of the works occupied by our division. A few nights since thirteen Yankees deserted & came over to us, thereby causing quite a vacant space in their piquet lines, Gen. Mahone observing this immediately sent into this space two regiments the 8th Florida and 11th Alabama, and swept their line for half a mile. The Yankeys thought they were being relieved. Over 250 prisoners were captured. So quickly and so easily was this done, that the two regiments with their prisoners were all within our works before the Yankeys knew it. Not a gun was fired from either side, until the Yankeys came out from their main line with a cheer & fired into their own rifle pits, expecting to find them full of "*rebels*", what must have been their chagrin at finding them empty. Among the prisoners was a soldier who had attempted to desert and had been caught and tied with a rope, and was condemned to be shot the following day. His cords were cut and he was released by our men, ought he not to be under everlasting obligations to Genl. Mahone? 'Tis said that one of the deserters, a Sergeant, piloted the Genl. into this space; if so he ought to receive as good a berth from us as possible. He must surely have been a true Southerner in principle or thoroughly sick and tired of fighting. I think they generally desert because they don't want to fight on *either* side.

Winter has come, and with it our sufferings have commenced. Every morning the ground is covered with thick white frost. For the past two or three days the wind has been blowing a perfect gale. There is no comfort at all standing round a fire built out of doors, which you know is the kind we have. Some of the soldiers have dug holes in the ground, and manage to keep themselves quite comfortable, if nothing calls them off. 'Tis said we will soon receive large tents, I don't believe it, tho', we've been promised that too often.

We have very good rations, but not nigh enough to soul & body together. A friend of mine, a Quarter Master, told me today he would give me a half bushel meal, if I would come to get it. I shall certainly go tomorrow.

Don't you suppose I will live high for awhile at least? There are only two of us in my mess, and we always eat up two days rations in one. You will, I've no doubt, *think* us very large eaters. Well, I should be surprised if you were not made confident of it, could you *see* us.

You will be surprised when I tell you we are again to have a new Brigadier. I. M. Sorrell, Longstreet's former Adjt. Genl. is expected to take command in a few days. All seem to be very well pleased with the appointment. I think, tho', 'tis treating Col. Gibson, our present commander, with very little respect. I think he is deserving the promotion. He will hardly remain with us, when Sorrell comes, I know if *I* were in his place, I shouldn't remain in the brigade.

This morning I received your last most interesting letter, and rest assured it relieved anxiety greatly; for I had been anxiously looking for several days. I had just concluded to wait no longer and had just taken my seat on the ground to write this letter. I have carefully read Senator Johnson's letter, an able and interesting production. I think he clearly puts forth the position of every true citizen of the Confederacy. Some may think from what he says we are yet to have many more years of hard fighting; but I still think peace will surely come in six months at farthest. I agree with the Senator in every thing except that portion relative to the election of the Yankey President. I believe we will have peace sooner by the election of Lincoln than by the election of McClellan. The former will fail to gain the support of the people & thereby cause a division, while the election of the latter will cause a uniting of the North, upon a new principle of conducting the war, and divide the South by offering peace upon a reconstruction of the Union. A great many would undoubtedly accede to such a proposition. So after all I've become to be a rabid Lincolnite, what do you think of it?

I am indeed glad to know that your neighborhood is again free from sickness. I think, tho', in leaving you it has made its way to us, as for the past week or so there has been quite a number of cases of fever & ague in *our* neighborhood. Nothing very serious, but very painful. Tell Babe she must get well. Keep up a cheerful spirit, and take lots of Quinine, she'll he all right.

I went to church in Petersburg this morning and listened to a most interesting sermon. I attended the Methodist church. There was quite a large congregation present. The church being in an exposed portion of the city and thereby subject to being struck by shells from the guns of the enemy, you would think it dangerous, at least imprudent for ladies to attend; but strange to say, it has so far been untouched. I attend almost every Sunday, when all is quiet along the lines.

For the past two or three days everything has been remarkably quiet until last night when an incessant sharp shooting and canonading was kept up during nearly the entire night. What was the cause or result I've not been able to learn. I presume it all arose from some one firing off his gun, thereby causing the whole line to fire. 'Twas very cold indeed, and' I think they might have been quiet a little while *at least*.

I wrote you sometime since that we had nothing to read. Since that time a public library has been opened in Petersburg for the benefit of our soldiery. By paying one dollar in advance, one can get a book by giving his name and keep it for ten days. He can thus get reading matter for a month. I think it quite a privilege don't you? I appreciate it very much and think 'tis very kind in some one to thus contribute to the happiness of our soldiers. I shall never forget them.

Our new Brigadier has just arrived and taken command of the brigade. He appears to be quite a nice man; but rather reserved, nothing like as fastidious as our present commander, Col. Gibson. I think tho' we will all get along pretty well. He is a real fancy fellow, rather tall and I must say *handsome*, if any *gentleman* can be such. Col. Gibson has tendered his resignation, and will in all probability leave us in a few days. He will carry with him the respect and esteem of the entire brigade.

I'm completely at a loss as to whom you have reference as having given you such a flattering description of Mother. I will give up that I can't guess who 'tis. Won't you tell me? I should like very much to know who 'tis. If 'tis not a Mr. Harrison, of Hayneville who formerly belonged to our regiment, I can't imagine it can be. He is the only one now remembered as having been at our house. I shall expect you to tell me the next time you write.

I am very glad indeed that you have promised to write every week at least as often as possible. You know I will do the *same*. I couldn't expect more from you, as your attention is necessarily very much engaged, while I have comparatively nothing to think about except *you*. So I hope we will hereafter receive letters more frequently from each other. I know 'twill be a great blessing to me.

My respects to all of your Father's family and all of my friends. With a hope of hearing from you soon and probably *seeing* you, I remain as ever yours affectionately and devotedly,

Alva

Millwood, Georgia
Dec. 11th 1864
Dearest Alva,

I was much rejoiced yesterday by the reception of your last most interesting letter dated 20th ult.

Owing to our line of communication having been interrupted by Sherman's army, I haven't heard from you before in it seems to me an age; and neigher have we heard one item of news from Virginia until a day or so past. The Post Office department has made new arrangements during the past week. Our line of communication is lengthened by the way of Albany and Thomasville which is the only alternative, till the central R. R. can be repaired.

I consider it unnecessary to write you the full particulars of Sherman's movement, since my last, as I guess you are kept as well posted as myself, if not better, although you are farther from the army than I am.

I have many times in my life wished Pa would sell out and move to middle Geo., as we would have the benefit of better schools and better society. Now I think about how thankful we should be that we are situated just where we are. It is the most safety place of refuge I can think of in this state. A great many refugees and exiles are flocking contin-ually to this county.

I do hope Sherman's army will not be permitted to make their escape in safety; but will all be captured or killed. I suppose they move very slowly in the direction of Savannah. I hope our force ahead is sufficient to meet them.

In my last I told you Pa had to go in service as Gov. Brown's[16] last call embraced his age. He reported at Macon, had two exemptions, his county office and mill consequently he was discharged. You haven't the least idea how rejoiced we were when he came. We had just sat down to supper table, when he drove in the yard and every one jumped up and ran to meet him, negroes, too. He hadent been gone more than three or four days. I don't know what we should do, if he should yet have to go, and not only our family but a great many others. He has to look to the interest of so many families.

John and Joe started to their command during Sherman's stay near Macon and were not permitted to go through, but in a few days were sent in company with a great many more Va. troops to Savannah by the lower rout, also the Militia went too. Aunt received a letter from them a few days since and they were still there, dident know when they should go on, probably not until some disposal is made of the Yanks near there.

---

[16] Georgia Governor Joseph E. Brown (1857-1865).

I'm truly glad to hear all "quiet about Petersburg" and that you have been permitted to go in winter quarters.

This is a dreadful cold day, I can scarcely write. I am constantly reminded of the uncomfortable condition of our soldiery. I wish you a pleasant time in your little cabin home. Yes, I do really think you ought to be permitted to spend Christmas in Geo. this year. I hope you may. I've been fearful, since the Yankees have destroyed the middle Geo. R.R. that may interfere with your expected visit to Dooly. I do not know whether any preparations are being made to repair the road now. I hope, though, there will be no preventative. I imagine if Genl. Sorrell, or at least think, if he approves, you will be successful in obtaining your furlough. Babe, Lou and Billy says they do wish Mr. Spencer would come to see us Christmas.

If I knew you could come then or near that time, I wouldn't write between now and then, I hope to hear again, soon from you. Pa knows of our engagement. I have not written at length. I hope to see you soon and tell you all the news. Emma Henry died last week with Typhoid fever. Amanda is now quite sick with the same. The family is in deep distress. All send love. With a hope of seeing you very soon, I am as ever, yours most devotedy, Mag.

CHAPTER SIX

1865

As this last year of the war begins, Alva, home on a furlough, has missed the first battle of the year. Rest assured he is not too disturbed by this as he returns to camp. In Margaret's home of Dooly County, communication to the north has been shut down except south through Thomasville and then east through Savannah. The 3rd Georgia engages the enemy trying stop an advance on the south side railroad at Hatcher's Run, Va., and Alva gives his account of General Sorrell being wounded by a stray mini-ball.

Things begin to slow down at this point in the war, with Alva's unit not seeing very much action. The communication lines are cut even further with the Union Army in Georgia, and the lack of mail and word from home takes it's toll. Apparently not all of the letters they exchanged were saved, however the ones we do have generally tell of camp life and Alva's thoughts on current events.

The last letter we have before Lee's surrender in Appomattox, at which Alva was present, was on March 24, 1865. The next one was written on July 10, 1865, and Alva writes from home in Penfield, describing the hard times the farmers are having as well as the now free slaves. Alva closes the letter by announcing he has taken the oath of allegiance.

Sunday at home
Jan. 8th 1865
Dearest Alva,

Communication has been open with Virginia two weeks, and not one word can I hear from you. What can be the cause, I can't conjecture. Every one most is receiving letters from their relatives and friends every mail day, but poor me can't get even *one* letter. My uneasiness and anxiety is constantly increased by the words that I hear every mail "no letter for you". I'm fearful you are seriously ill, or some other misfortune has happened to you. You have always been so punctual during our long correspondence that I'm confident there is some valid reason for your silence. I have made many excuses for you, but don't know which if any are correct.

Your last dated 20th November was rec'd. the first Dec. which I answered in a few days after its' reception. Communication was then only open by the way of Thomasville and Savannah and in a short time the Yankees took possession of a portion of the road thereby preventing us from learning any news whatever from Va. for four or five weeks. Of course I didn't expect any letters during that time, but since the old line of communication has been reestablished I have and have been sadly disappointed by not receiving any. I could have written much earlier than this, but as you expected a furlough this winter, I thought I would wait till I heard from you again, as you might doubtless be in Georgia before a letter could reach you. I promised myself last week, if I didn't hear from you yesterday, I would write any way though I hardly know what to write you for fear you will not receive this letter. I believe I will not write at length probably you will come to see us this week and that would certainly give us more pleasure than 20 letters. I have much to tell you about our merry Christmas. You haven't the least idea what a nice time we have had. I have said "we". I will retract for *I* have been rather melancholy, simply because you have not written to me. But I do think some enjoyed themselves finely. There were several parties in the neighborhood. I attended them. One Cotillion, of course I was only an observer at that. One riding party, on horseback; one social or conversation party. I have many interesting jokes to tell you on Samantha and Babe, and will do so when I see you.

Sure enough Sherman has reached the coast. I believe he can go any where he pleases. Some predict that he will take Augusta next. I hope this letter will go through first. I'm about to despair of our ever gaining our independence. We have had so many reverses of late. I still think this spring, the struggle will be decided. Let our fate be what it may, I want to see it. I wish the suspense to be done away with.

John and Joe are in S. C. near Charleston, but think they will soon be sent to their command in Va.

We have received but one letter from Brother since he was captured. Excuse this hastily written and uninteresting letter. I don't know how to write, think it doubtful whether you will receive it. Will I be disappointed this week? I hope not.

As ever yours faithfully and devotedly,
Mag

Penfield
Jany. 25th 1865
Dearest Maggie,

Tomorrow is my last day at home, and it is indeed sad to think that I am so soon to leave, perhaps *never* to return. Today I have been busy entertaining friends, and packing up a box of eatables. I thought 'twouldn't do to commence *starving* so soon after getting into camp.

I will be accompanied by a member of my company who is now at home on furlough. I have several boxes to carry for different members of the company and *know* I will be much troubled; but *hope* I shall get along well.

I commenced this several hours ago; but have been interrupted by Dr. Morgan and lady who came to bid good bye to "Ab", as I am called by almost every one in town. I do not intend this for a *letter*, 'tis merely a *note*, telling that I am *almost* gone and that although I am far away, I still think of you.

I desired very much to have heard from you, before I *left*; but I knew that was impossible, still I couldn't help wishing it. It seems almost an age since I heard from you. I hope, however, 'twill not be long first.

You know I do not wish to leave home; but I hear so many discouraging reports, and see so many whipped men I'm *almost crazy*. 'Tis a shame on Georgia that so *many* are actually in favor of reconstruction. I have no sympathy with such, and can *almost* be rejoiced at any calamity that befalls them. 'Tis indeed, poor encouragement to our armies. Some are *determined* to be subjugated, whether or no. I say shame on all such.

I wish I had *time* to write you a letter Maggie; but just wait until I get *home*, and I will write you a long letter. From all accounts, I expect I shall be travelling eight or nine days; if so, I expect your next, will be received soon after my arrival. I sincerely hope so.

I expect to leave tomorrow morning early, and I know I have your heartfelt desires for my safe and speedy arrival in camp. I will write so soon' as I stop and try and interest you with a description of my journey.

All are well, and send love. My respects to *all* your Father's family, "Sis", "Aunt Nancy", Eliza and Betty.

Fannie sends love.

Rest assured, you have, as ever, the pure love, of thine own devoted

Alva

P.S. I will mail this "en route".

A.

("Fannie" is Alva's sister, Julia Frances Spencer)

Camp Sorrel's Brigade
Feby. 4th 1865
Dearest Maggie,

I am once more safely in camp, after having undergone the most disagreeable hardship I ever experienced. Just think of my being on the road since the morning of the 26th. I missed connection at the first depot, and at every other junction between Georgia and Virginia. I arrived in camp with my boxes and am now enjoying their contents. True I was subjected to a great deal of trouble; but I'm now more than doubly compensated. I found the most substantial things sent me before I left for home, saved for me. The groceries were eaten by my friends with both dispositions I was perfectly satisfied, especially with the former. I found my brigade just returned from another raid in the direction of Weldon. They were very much fatigued, and represented the trip as having been much more severe than the former. I was fortunate in missing it, don't you think so? They were very thankful for my small contribution to their "commissary department". They are not half so badly supplied with provisions as some have represented. They are not *suffering*, to say the least. And above all, they are not whipped. While the *people* (a part of them) are ready for reconstruction. The soldiers are very much displeased with the "situation" of affairs in Georgia, and I expect *some of them*, will receive some "raking" documents.

You know, I wrote you that I expected to be accompanied by a lady to Charlotte N.C. *Fortunately*, I was detained twenty four hours the first day I left home. She becoming impatient, left Augusta the morning before my arrival. I was never more glad at anything. I was surely *deprived* of a great deal of trouble.

The first question I was asked when I entered camp was are you married? I didn't know *that* was so generally the custom of soldiers, til I returned to the army. One of my friends from Wilkinson county, entered the "holy state", and has not returned. I'm afraid he will be summarily punished. I reported to Gen. Sorrel, and gave him a full description of my travels, and the unavoidable delays to which I was subjected. He was perfectly satisfied, and enquired very particularly how I enjoyed myself and if I succeeded in getting my boxes safely through. He only regretted that all couldn't have returned at the expiration of their furloughs and all have come together. Five of our members are still behind, and we have nothing to do until all have returned. Not having anything to do makes me more homesick and gloomy than ever.

So, soon as I arrived in camp, I enquired if there were any letters for me. I received three, two from home, and one from you. Although 'twas old, 'twas nevertheless acceptable, and read with great pleasure. So you needn't be afraid that the Yankeys read it.

I can very easily appreciate your feelings, when you thought I was sick. I've experienced the same several times since the present campaign was inaugurated. I can very easily imagine your joy when my unexpected visit dispelled such gloomy thoughts. It surely gave me great pleasure; but my grief at parting, I can never forget; so far from it, that I have and still undergo many gloomy moments. I know I ought to dispel all such thoughts; but tis impossible. I couldn't however s much I desired it, really 'tis a relief and great pleasure to revisit the many happy hours we've so recently experienced in each others' society. May such a happy time again speedily return.

Upon my arrival in camp I found that on account of the scarcity of wood, our houses had been completely destroyed, and I am reduced to the necessity of *seeking refuge* elsewhere. I am staying with my company, and am getting along finely. We have a very good cook and are therefore not greatly troubled with household affairs. I intend staying here until I can get a tent.

By a casual glance at this sheet, you will see that it has been somewhat soiled. During dinner I accidentally let some butter fall on it. That's a good way I have of telling you we had a good dinner. I believe I will tell you our prospects for living. We have one ham, two middlings, several pounds of sausage, six or eight pounds of butter, forty or fifty pounds of flour, one half bushel peas, one jar pickles and one bottle vinegar. There are four of us in a mess. Besides our regular rations, we have the above. Don't you think we can make out for awhile. I think so, at least for a week or so.

Several members of my company gave me glowing descriptions of the feast they had of my *turkey*. I though at that time was enjoying myself much more pleasantly with *you*. I know they enjoyed themselves finely. I haven't quite forgotten how I *used* to feel on such occasions.

I had hoped Maggie, to have received one of your dear letters before this, but can't reasonably expect one in several days yet. I can't help but look for one. Rest assured, I shall write *often*, whether I receive yours or not, I know, for you've promised you will do the same. I shall look for a long one in a few days. All well.

My respects to your Father's family, Sis, Mr. H. & my enquiring friends. I've seen Miss Milas' uncle; he's well.

Rest assured I am thine own devoted.

Alva

Winter Quarters Sorrel's Brigade
Feby 10th 1865
Dearest Maggie,

Instead of peace, you will ere this reaches you, see that again the two opposing armies around Petersburg have met in deadly conflict. Sunday evening, with only a few minutes warning, our entire division was moving towards our right. Late in the afternoon, the enemy was met in small force and driven from the field with a very slight loss to us. One member of my company was slightly wounded. About twelve oclock on Monday our Division received orders to return to camp. They came within a mile of our quarters when they were ordered back and met the enemy about seven miles distant. Our brigade, indeed the Division, are said to have acted with unprecedented gallantry driving the enemy from every point, capturing their entire works. The entire loss on the Brigade will reach near eighty or one hundred. About seventy-five were wounded and ten or twelve killed.

Out of this number, forty were wounded from our Regt., and five or six killed. My company lost ten wounded, none mortally, none killed. My confidant and best friend[1] will lose his left arm between the elbow and shoulder. It does indeed make me feel sad to see so many of my friends falling around me. Oh for something to stop this destructive conflict.

Today is sleeting and raining, and while the balance of my comrades are exposed to all the hardships of the storm, and dangers of the battle field, I am permitted to remain in camp. I am greatly blessed and am truly thankful to a good and just God for his many, many mercies. I sometimes think am I worthy of such great blessings! And fear that I am not. I am resolved that God helping me, I will hereafter live more for his honor and glory, and the advancement of this cause on earth. I know I haven't been a Christian, doing many things that I ought not to have done, and failing to do many that I should have done; but I believe God helping me and the prayers of those who love me will affect such a change in my life; that I will be a far better person, and far better prepared to die when God calls me. Dearest Maggie, will you, when you breathe your secret prayer to God, sometimes, ask that we may still be permitted to live, to make ourselves happy, and to glorify his holy name? And if that is not con-sistent with his holy will, Oh petition that *I* may be permitted to enter that Heaven above, where, I know, you and all the redeemed of God will be. I do not write this gloomily, Maggie, because I've heard or seen anything in our country's condition calculated to produce such a state of mind; but because I am so much mortified at my past conduct, and am so firmly resolved to persue a different course. I have been extremely wicked and 'tis this that causes one to feel so very, very sad and gloomy.

The "Peace Commissioners" have returned, telling us "the argument is exhausted, let us stand by our arms". They were permitted to go no nearer Washington than Fortress Monroe, at which place they were met by inhuman Lincoln, and the subtle

---

[1] Beleived to be Benjamin F. Barnwell.

intreguer Seward. Nothing was accomplished, save our Commissioners being told they were rebel traitors, and deserved to be hung (which they had been told before). After this *polite* and *startling* information, they were *respectfully* informed "they could return to *Rebeldom*", old "*Abe*" remarking "God bless you Hunter". Thus endeth the Peace question, "*peace* to its ashes". I hope no *sensationist* will again revive it. I think we all can now see what is the character of our enemies. We can do nothing but await the time when we shall be more powerful than they. To insure such an event, we have but to put forth every energy, in the field and at home. The people must encourage the army and all will be well. We have virtually commenced a *new war*. It does look gloomy; but contrast independence with submission or subjugation. Let every man's motto be "Liberty or death", and independence is ours.

Pres. Davis has said that, "Lincoln signified his willingness to receive and treat with commissioners"; instead of that, what has he done, but insulted our nation, and shown to us that the true policy of the Yankey government was the complete annihilation of the entire Southern Confederacy. We can look forward for no aid, save from a good and just God, and our own natural inherent resources. Let us earnestly seek the former, and advantageously use the latter. Don't despond, Maggie, but keep up a brave heart, always looking forward to a brighter, happier time. I have told my comrades, the *ladies* of Georgia, were not whipped if *some* of the *men* were. I know *you* are not an exception. If you remain hopeful and cheerful you know not what a great encouragement 'twill be to me. I know you have lost near and dear relatives; but oh remember that if all despond, soon *all* may be lost and swallowed up in Yankey "rule and ruin". What will home, friends, country be worth if we submit. We will be subject to untold indignities and slaves to Yankey masters and mistresses in worse than Egyptian bondage. None are more desirous to obtain peace than I. I have an object to attain to, which would make me forget all the many, many hardships I've undergone and render me the happiest among men. If we could gain anything by reconstruction, *I* would willingly give my consent; but we all know that instead of gaining, we would lose *everything*. We would be the "laughing stock" of the whole civilized world, and be reduced to such an extremity as to be compelled to beg for the common every day necessaries of life.

Since I wrote the within, I've received additional information from the field, to the effect that our commander, Genl. Sorrel is mortally wounded. He was sitting behind our works, and was shot through the right lung by a stray ball. Doesn't it look hard that after going through a severe engagement unhurt, one should receive a mortal wound. Our brigade commanders are surely unfortunate. I try tho to think 'tis for the best. We are not sure that the Genl. is mortally wounded, we very much fear 'tis so. Just as we had become acquainted with him, he is taken from us. I know nothing of his preparation for death, I only hope he will be (should he die) at rest. Not a more perfect gentleman or a more gallant soldier ever lived. His loss will be greatly felt and mourned. Genl. Sorrel is improving and 'tis pretty generally believed he will recover. All the wounded are getting along, fine. This morning's paper states that the enemy have succeeded in cutting the R.R. between Augusta and Branchville; if so, I know I shall be perfectly -------- to Vienna.

Every one who receives a furlough, I hope will carry a letter for you. I haven't recd. a letter from you since I returned to camp, and I assure you I'm almost miserable. I shall continue to look until I'm certain that the Yankeys have the R.R. Will you please dearest Maggie write *every* opportunity? I know you will.

Should we be, so unfortunate as to never hear from each other again, rest assured, I will always remember you in love. Love to all your Father's family & friends.

Yours as ever devotedly.

Alva

P.S. I send this by the Sergt. Maj. of our Regt. to be mailed somewhere in Georgia.

Alva

Winter Quarters, Sorrel's Brigade
Feby. 17th 1865
Dearest Maggie,
Although I've recently written to you, I cannot *now*, as there is a strong probability of being prevented altogether, fail to tell you farewell. The sadness I now feel is inexpressible, and can be equalled only by the heart-rending pangs I suffered when I so recently parted with you in person.

This life is not all sunshine and pleasure, as we both have already learned. 'Tis chequered with many and varied scenes of unhappy all this gloom and sadness.

Secretly oer the darkest doom
There shines some ling'ring beam of gladness.

True 'tis soothing to be thus buoyed up by such a fond hope; but I've learned *too* well that *such* are, "Like rainbow joys that end in weeping".

In the past, Maggie, our privileges have been great. Never, except for a very short time, since the commencement of our correspondence, have we been deprived the inestimable privilege of regularly hearing from each other. Others have been debarred this priceless *boon*, almost during the whole of the present struggle. Now that 'tis probable that we, too, are to be subject to a like fate, it does indeed render me sad and gloomy. Not that I think the separation will be for a great while or that absence and silence will conquer the love of either for the other; but because 'twill be so *painful* to be separated for *however* short a time. I know that whatever be our fate you will prove true, and that when we *do* meet again, I will receive that same pure affection with which I'm now so loth to part. I can not prove to you, the purity and unchangeableness of my love more clearly than I have already done so frequently before. I can only say:

Remember in absence, in sorrow and pain
There's *one* heart, unchanging, that beats but for thee.

I know 'twill be painful to but I trust we will calmly resign ourselves to whatever fate befalls us. We think, upon the approach of *any* misfortune, that we can't bear it; but "The human heart *can* suffer. It can hold more tears than the ocean holds waters. We never know-how deep, how wide it is, until misery begins to unbind her clouds, and fills it with rushing blackness".

I have the same story to tell you, no letter *yet*. I have given up all hope of hearing from you again.

I'm now about to make a request of you, Maggie, which I'm afraid you will consider *very* unbecoming; but, for one *moment*, consider my great anxiety and almost insupportable suspense, and I believe you will not only comply, but excuse my seeming impropriety. Belonging to a command from Middle Georgia, I have no hope whatever of receiving letters by soldiers at home on furlough. To surmount this difficulty, will you write me *one* more long, long letter, and enclose it in a letter to Sister Fannie, requesting her to forward it by some one coming on to the Army of Virginia? I will surely get it. This may be the *last* opportunity and you know not *how* anxious I am to hear from you *once* more. By sending it immediately upon the reception of this, 'twill be brought on to me by a member of this company who left for home this morning. I hope you will comply this *one* time, and if you cannot *continue*, I shall be satisfied *necessarily*, for awhile at least.

Mother ---- since I last wrote. Everything remains quiet. No prospect of a speedy movement. Our wounded are getting along finely. Genl. Sorrel is thought to be out of danger.

Sherman, contrary to my expectation, seems to be marching on to Columbia. If he is successful, all communication, by any means, will be effectually destroyed, for *awhile* at least. That he will be successful, I haven't the least idea. His laurels will all be turned to weeping willows.

Love to all. With a fond hope of hearing from you *very* soon, I must bid you good bye. Continue dearest Maggie to think of me as your devoted.

Alva

P.S. This will be mailed in Macon by a friend of mine belonging to the 48th Ga. who will leave in the morning. A.

At Home, Georgia
Feby. 17th 1865
Dearest Alva,

As I anticipated the detestable Yankees have cut the road at or near Branchville, but however slight may be the probability of your receiving a letter, I will write. One week has elapsed since the road was interrupted, but I don't know whether they still hold possession or not; as I haven't seen a paper in several days, neither have I heard any late news from that point; though I hope the road has been repaired and communication is again open to Virginia.

A great many troops are being sent to S.C. the greater portion of Hood's army. I suppose/are there, and he at his own request has been relieved of the command. No doubt a general engagement will take place soon, and I hear our troops are sanguine of success. I sincerely hope we may be successful, and that we may never have another reversal during the continuance of this cruel, cruel war. Since our Coms have returned and informed the people of the result of their interview with the Federal Coms, I hope now the urgent request "Send Coms to negotiate with the Federal Government" will cease, and that such a dishonorable proposition for peace, will not have a discouraging effect upon our soldiers and the people at home, but to the contrary, will unite and inspire them with redoubled energy to fight on, fight ever, rather than submit to Yankee rule and oppression. I confess, I did hope some honorable proposition would be made that we could accept of though I didn't hardly think there would be consequently I was not much disappointed, when I heard upon what conditions we could have peace with them. Before our Coms returned I heard a great many predict that the last battle had been fought and that peace and happiness would soon reign over our now distracted country. Though I never was so certain as to talk or believe thus. Unless we can form alliance with some foreign power, I see but ---- before us, fight, fight ever. There is much talk now of arming the slaves and putting them in service and every one I believe think it a good idea. If they will fight, of course, 'twill be a great help, but generally, they are such cowards. I fear they will not be of much benefit to our army. Pa says he doesn't believe he has one that will volunteer and fight for his freedom. But I hope whatever is done, will work for the best. I know I'm very, very tired of the war, and I know too, as long as it continues my dear Brother will be confined in a northern prison subject to sickness and insults, and *you* exposed to danger, hardships and sickness, all of which keeps my mind in a state of great anxiety and fear. We've recd. a letter from Brother since I wrote you, but 'twas of an old date, written two months ago, then he was well, and desired very much for Ma to send him a box, to contain clothing and tobacco. He is very anxious to hear from home, has never heard a word since his capture, though he said, he had written several times. I wrote him last week, I hope 'twill reach him. He is at Point-Lookout.

I heard today there has been a fight recently at Petersburg, we repulsed the enemy with loss of 500, the loss on the enemies side considerable. I hope I get a long letter tomorrow from you, but if I should be disappointed, how *sad I will be*.

Yours written the day before your leave of your home, was recd. in a few days afterward 'twas not delayed as the other was. I was truly glad to receive it, but was sad, indeed, to know that you were gone again *so far* distant from home, friends, and her, who loves you more than all others. Your visit, though *so* short, it seems more like a dream than a reality, doubly increased my love (if possible) for you, and 'tis indeed sad thought that a year and perhaps two, will elapse before we can again see each other.

I wish you could see a letter I recd. from Mrs. Everett since I saw you. She said the day you takened the train you looked very sad, and had but little to say. She wanted to know what did I tell you to make you thus, that if I had jilted with you, she hoped I would never have the chance of another Spencer. You seemed to have her sympathies but she gave me "particular" all through the letter. I've not replied yet, but when I do, will let her know or at least give her a hint, that she is under a wrong impression. I believe I'll pretend that I've not had an opportunity to treat you thus yet. She thinks you are a "powerful clever, kind, nice little soldier". I also rec'd. a letter from my cousin Mrs. Payne a few days since, telling me about Mr. Payne having made your acquaintance on his return from Athens.

She had many questions to ask, as had not heard from her before in a long time. She intends visiting us this summer.

Babe has just returned from school this evening, and says tell you she is highly pleased with her new teacher, Miss Alden. She boards at Mr. Brown's 1 1/2 miles from the school-house. She is sent every morning in company with Mr. B.'s daughter to the school house in a little "jersey wagon", and then sent for in the afternoon. She says she has such a nice time.

Louisa and the little Boys are ---- to Mrs. Andrews again this year, but Little Bud Steel's ---- on us about every other morning, he doesn't like to go at all, says it's too much trouble to walk so far, that if Ma will let him stay at home till he gets as large as Jimmie Graham he will then go all the time. He starts off every morning with the rest, but when he gets to Aunt Nancy's stops and won't go any further, comes about 12 oclock home, looking as if he had done all that was required of him. There is no school at Millwood.

Oh I was invited to a party at Miss Pounds tonight, but I'd thought such a little about it, I almost forgot to tell you, 'tis a surprise party, I suppose. I think it rather late for them now and don't care to attend no way. All send love. As ever yours affectionately and devotedly.

Mag

P.S. You know not how anxiously I look for a letter today 18th inst. I *do hope* I will not be disappointed. I send this off in a few minutes, with the hope that it may soon reach you.

Mag

At Home, Georgia
Feby 24th 1865
Dearest Alva,

Last evening I was most agreeable surprised by the reception of your most interesting letter of the 4th inst. Having heard that communications were cut off, I greatly feared a long long time would elapse before I would again have the happy pleasure of hearing from you. I was almost afraid to expect a letter, lest I should be disappointed; but I'm truly glad my supposition was wrong, that Sherman has *not* accomplished that which he so much desires, and I so hope he may never be permitted to destroy effectually the communication. It is really amusing sometimes here to witness our *tiptoe expectation* for the arrival of mail. Yesterday evening company came in. Mrs. Rice, a widowed sister of Miss Julia's, Sis, Anne, and Mr. Woodson, the gentleman who boarded here last year, and is now on his way to join his command in Macon. While at supper Ma told us she would send to the Office, perhaps Mr. H. had brought out the weeks mail, though she didn't hardly think we would receive any news from Virginia whatever, and neither did I. After supper we all assembled in the parlor around the fire, more cheerful, you know, for the piece that feeds the flame, each one seemed to be asking, I wonder if I will get a letter? Sis was very anxious to hear from her brothers as she hadn't heard in some time. Mrs. Rice, says, "Well,

Puss, are you not expecting a letter? I dreamed last night of seeing you reading a letter from some one, you wouldn't tell whom; written with very black ink on white paper". I told her I was not, but I hoped she would realize her dream tonight. In the course of a short time I heard some one walk in Ma's room. I noiselessly stepped out into her room and she was emptying the contents of the mail sachel, which was full. We said nothing to those in the parlor, till we looked over all. Then I walked in, said, mail's come, "lots" of it. All were in such a state of anxiety they could scarcely wait for me to distribute the letters. Every one had a letter but Mr. W. who of course did not expect any. You can imagine what a pleasant time we all had reading them. Sis rec'd. three from her brothers, Samantha one from her cousin, Mrs. R. one from her aunt, and I told them mine was from *my cousin*. No one knew any better, unless "twas Samantha. Company has all left this morning except Mr. W. who will leave perhaps this evening. Samantha is entertaining him, though she's not displeased because I've left her alone. She's just come to me and said, "Puss please go in the parlor, I don't want to stay in there." I told her she must entertain her beaus, that I could not. I think he's rather smitten, but S. doesn't care a straw for him. I can tease her so much about him. If you remember I told you he sent her a piece of music, "No One to Love". He's a great lover of music, and not more than 19 or 20 years old, not near grown I suppose.

Well something else now. I'm truly glad you arrived safely in camps with your boxes. You certainly had a most disagreeable trip. Soldiers going from her won't carry anything back for their friends, owing to the conditions of the roads. I know it must be very troublesome to carry boxes through , but of course one hates to refuse knowing how they appreciate such a favor from others. I'm glad you have so much "good eating". As the little boy said, I really think "you *are* well off to live" particularly as long as it last. The people seem to be very uneasy about the condition of Gen'l. Lee's army, lest it should suffer for provisions. We cannot hear any news from S.C. whatever. The movements of the two armies are kept secret for some purpose. I hope Sherman will get a good whipping whenever he makes an attack.

I've seen a few telegraphic dispatches from Richmond concerning the fight, around Petersburg. Gen'l. Sorrel was wounded and Gen'l. Pegram was killed. Sis had one letter from John dated the 7th inst. up to which time he hadn't participated in any engagements. I hope they were not engaged in any since. John says he is more anxious to see home than ever before and he can't imagine the cause. Joe, I think is satisfied any where, he's been exposed to so much hardship suffering and danger, that he's become reckless.

You know I wrote you that Mr. Deaton's family were expecting a soldier friend to visit them this month. Today they rec'd a letter from him. He's at his home in Macon, but can't visit them. I guess they are rather disappointed as they intended to send young Mr. T. a box by him, though he has promised if they will send it up he will carry it to him.

I delivered your message to Mollie. She ask me to show her your letter, but I refused. Ma was to see Mrs. D. this week and Mollie sent word for me not to write to you before she saw me, that she wanted to send some word. I've not seen her yet, consequently I don't know what she wished me to write. She firmly believes we are engaged. Several times she's talked around Aunt N. and Samantha to find out.

She and John G. corresponds, but you mustn't let him know that you know it, for he would suspicion me at once of telling you. I guess 'tis no more than a friendly correspondence.

I've not had an opportunity of going to Macon yet but hope I will soon. Pa has to go up soon. I fully intend to comply with my promise if possible. I sent a piece of gold to a Jewelry shop a few days since to be made into rings. I guess twill make two rings. One I intend to give to you.

I will send it to you in a letter if I think twill go safely, when I get them home.

Well I wrote you last week and have written this week. I reckon Mr. H. will think, well a letter every week to him! hem!

Remember my love to Fannie when you write home. All are well and send love. Rest assured I am your devoted.

Maggie

In the trenches between the James and the Appomattox rivers.
March 6th 1865
Dearest Maggie,
A few days since I received your last most interesting letter, and you can't imagine how great a change it produced in my feelings. I had almost concluded that I shouldn't hear from you again, and you can easily imagine how great and agreeable was the surprise. You seemed to think that I had become vexed with you because of your inability to fulfil your promise, do you, Maggie, think me so ungenerous as to be offended at your failure to accomplish that which is impossible? True I was sadly disappointed for indeed I know nothing I would rather possess than that. I did not, however, in my disappointment, a single moment blame you. I *knew* you had done every thing in your power; for you had told me so. You ask me, in what way I preferred having it sent. If is is entirely suitable with you, I prefer having it sent to Fannie who can send it directly to me. You can however suit your own convenience and pleasure. The quickest way will suit me best. In one of my recent letters, I requested you to write to me, through Sister. I shall therefore look for a letter from you by a member of my company now at home on furlough. I don't believe you will have any objection to our correspondence through that medium. I assure you that Fannie (although she's my sister) is a good girl, and although she has never seen you, she loves you for my sake, and will do anything she can to promote our mutual happiness. She says "your letters breathe such purity and loveliness" that she knows you must be all I've represented.

I should like very much to attend a party in Dooly; but you know that when I was last at your home 'twas impossible for me to have remained any longer. I am glad you didn't insist on my staying, for I should have very much disliked to have refused. You will see by the caption of this letter that we've again been moving. We now occupy the lines recently occupied by Picketts' Division. We only hope to remain here. We are tired of running about on the right of our lines. Here although the lines are near enough each other, to see the men on the works from one line to the other, there is not much probability of an engagement. We may have severe artillery duels; but then we have very good protection. So after all this is much the more preferable position. I think tho' will leave here soon.

Once more I've heard from home. This is the first time since I left. The cause of the delay having been so great was the gentleman who brought the letters was stopped in Augusta; he went back home and came round through the country, he was about 20 days on the road. I'm expecting letters by other members of the company now at home. Their time is out long since.

I wish I had time to write more, Maggie, but the gentleman who will carry this expects to leave now in a little while. I hope you will receive it, not that I think 'twill be of any interest; but merely to let you know I'm well, etc. My love to all your Father's family & Miss Sis. Write often as you can.

Ever yours most devotedly,
Alva

Sorrel's Brigade
Mch. 10th 1865
Dearest Maggie,

I have but a few minutes in which to write and I'm writing by a very dim fire light. I don't expect you can read it but I will write a few lines. I wrote to you some few days since, to be carried by a paroled prisoner going home; but when he arrived in Petersburg, he was not permitted to go any further, being told he was exchanged, whereupon he mailed them. I don't suppose you will ever get them.

In your last, you requested me to inform you in what manner I preferred your ambrotype being sent, I would prefer, as you proposed, to have it sent to Sister Fannie, who will forward it to me by some member of the company now at home on furlough. You know, though, Maggie, I wish you to do as *you* think best, not *I*. In the mean time, I shall continue to look for it. A day or two since I recd. letters from home, and being the first since my return to duty, you can easily imagine how highly they were appreciated. Speaking of receiving letters, reminds me that a day or two since I recd. a *very nice* valentine from someone in Ga. (I think I know who). If the sentiments therein expressed are the true ones of she who sent it (and I doubt not they are), I'm very sorry that I inflicted pain upon anyone upon parting, and am also flattered to know that I'm "held so dear" by the fair one who sent it. As 'twas mailed in *your* county, probably you will oblige me by giving *her* my sincere thanks.

We are now on the line between the James & the Appomattox rivers. We occupy the position formerly held by Picket's Division. We are very well situated. Although we can see the Yanks (about a thousand yards off) we do not expect an engagement. We may, however, be subject to a shelling occasionally. *I will try and take care of myself.* My light is about out so I must close. Love to all. Write as often as you see any prospect of my receiving it.

As ever yours most devotedly,
Alva

Camp of Sorrel's Brigade, A. N. V.
March 24th 1865
Dearest Maggie,
'Tis with pleasure I commence this letter, for I feel less despondent than when I last wrote to you, and therefore I'm not fearful of causing you unnecessary pain or fear as to the successful and speedy termination of all the difficulties now threatening our destruction.

We have often made predictions as to the end and have so far been woefully disappointed, too painfully being made aware the fact that we were not prophets.

It has been said that "Disappointment treads on the heels of Hope, and extenguishes in despair the light which had dazzled in anticipation", but does our failure to have all our desires gratified cause despair? Not at all. After every reverse that has happened to our arms, there has been a cloud of *gloom* cast over us; but not despair. Each time, we have looked upon the "bright side", renewing our determination to be free and resolving to prevent a repetition of the disaster. It does seem as if our danger now were greater than ever; but let us recollect that as our strength has decreased, that of the enemy has been far greater, and that to day, we are as equal to the emergency as ever. I see no cause for despondency; but on the contrary, I think there is great encouragement to *hope*.

Sherman has gone almost unopposed through the most flourishing portions of the Confederacy; but has he conquered the people? True, his progress will have a deleterious effect upon our cause abroad; but 'tis far from "crushing the rebellion, as our motley inferiors across the waters would make us believe. In one of my letters, I told you I thought his (Sherman's) laurels would soon be turned into weeping willows, that day, I honestly believe, is now dawning. The repulse of our Peace Commissioners, has also produced a desirable effect, causing a greater unanimity of feeling to exist among our people than ever before. The "Negro" bill has been passed, and already the negroes are being put into the field. This will undoubtedly greatly increase our effective force, since the places of many of our troops now occupying the lines around Petersburg and Richmond can be easily filled; but I think this bill unconstitutional and violently antagonistical to the principles for which we are fighting; if however, 'tis reported to as an act of necessity I cheerfully acquiesce. These men being relieved can operate more successfully upon the enemy's flanks, and soon we would be ready for another foray into Pennsylvania. I know what you will say to *this*, since you've already told me, you were "opposed to invasion"; but I believe thats the only way to make Yankeys cry "enough". 'Tis certainly better for us to enter the enemy's country, and be fed by them, than remain in these detestable ditches poorly provided for, subject to every manner of disease and to death from the many and fiendish invasions of our foe. More men have been lost since we came south of Richmond than in the celebrated battle of Gettysburg.

I'm glad to learn that Senator Hill and others are delivering addresses to the people of Georgia; for I am sorry to say I think they need some stimulus to make them do their duty, since they will not do it voluntarily. NOW is the times we need their encouragement and their strongest efforts. Why do they withhold it? Surely they do expect to save anything by submission or reconstruction. On the contrary, they will lose everything, not even their home will be spared.

The celebrated Yankey raider Sheridan is doing some damage in North Western and Western Virginia; but 'twill not always be so, our time will come next.

I will try and give you a description of our situation since I've told you all I know about that of our country. We have three houses. Two we made of pine logs, and are surrounded by a very thick bank of dirt to protect them from shells and minnie balls. One of these two is occupied by a very eccentric personage, who is constantly a source of enjoyment on account of his witty remarks and strange notions. In this dirt surrounding our houses, the rats have burrowed, and at night they make very destructive forays upon one's rations. A night or two since that eccentric person of whom I've spoken, was very much annoyed by their running across his feet. One more bold than the others made an attack, whereupon a kick was made, and he supposes he threw him into his nest, as nothing was afterwards heard from him. He thinks they are trying Grant's plan (undermining) and is constantly in dread of being "blown up". *My* house is made entirely of boards set upright against posts set into the ground. We were told by those whom we relieved that 'twas built for a summer house and I answer admirably, I assure you. Being built in this style (if style it be), there is very little room for them (the rats) to hide; but we have a few *little* fellows (which are not customarily honored with the dignified appelation of R.A.T.S.) that are a source of some annoyance; but fortunately our rations so far have been spared. *We* are the enemies to that portion of our possessions, as they invariably fail to last the length of time for which they are drawn.

March has come and nearly gone rest assured there are none here who desire its return. I've never in my life experienced such disagreeable wintry weather. It has almost been unsafe for one to venture out of his cabin, for fear of endangering his eye sight, or irremediably losing his hat, which, these *hard* times, is of *much* the greatest value. Some nights we have layed down expecting, before morning , to wake up and find our house gone. That beats Georgia winds, doesn't it? You would have laughed to have seen us (myself and three others composing my "mess") propping our house to prevent its falling.

The buds of spring—"those beautiful harbingers of sunny skies and cloudless times"—begin to make their appearance and the warbling blue bird merrily singing forms a strange contrast to the scenes of which we've so recently been witnesses. Everything possesses new life and beauty and the lovely beauties of Nature *now* unfolded to us, in a slight degree compensates for our separation from those we love.

Since we cannot find that sympathy, for which the heart so much longs, from the society of our fellow soldiers, we have recourse to the soothing influences of the ripling water, the carolling bird and the whispering zephyr. We no longer feel the rough cold blast of winter, but the blue canopies, the glittering streams, the green fields and the life-imparting breezes of nature are "beauty to the eye and music to the ear."

The (18th) of March was one which we will not soon forget on account of its having been so different from our usual "life." On that day, the citizens of Petersburg, presented to Genl. Mahone (our division commander) a handsome sword for his gallant conduct during the war & especially during the last campaign. A day or two previous to the presentation a congratulatory order to the Division was read, also one detailing (800) men to be present at the *presentation*. One of the committee presented it, whereupon Genl. M. responded in a neat and very appropriate address. This sword is said to have cost three thousand dollars.

On the (19th) I went down our lines to the James, and from the celebrated "Howlett" battery I had a splendid view of the Yankey boats, batteries, "Dutch gap" canal, and our lines on the north side of the river. The Yankeys have an observatory very near our works between two hundred and fifty and three hundred feet high, and strange to say our artillery, so far, has been unable to touch it. From this observatory nearly our whole line can be seen. I could very plainly see the Yankey in the top of it waving his signal flag. I could see a Yankey regiment of negroes on piquet just below and not far from Howlett's battery. Several squads of paroled prisoners were seen marching up the river towards Richmond and a similar number of Yankeys were seen coming from the above place. Oh, I do hope *all* our prisoners will soon return and be permitted to go home, for a short time, at least. A great many of my acquaintances have returned and some of my company. We received a letter from our Captain (Sanders) a few days since, who expects soon to be exchanged. Our Colonel, Lt. Colonel and Major are already at home.

It has been such a long, long time since I heard from you, I know not how to content myself. Nothing gives me any permanent enjoyment. "Tis only momentary and soon, I find my thoughts wandering to you, and other dear ones at home. If you could see us sometimes, after the excitement (caused by some brilliant war news) had worn off, sitting huddled over a few coals of fire, each "wrapt in the solitude of his own imagination" you would think we were indeed holding a Quaker meeting. In a few moments, however, the silence is broken by some one exclaiming "Oh goodness! I wish I was at home"; but no reply being made in vain, I try to concentrate my thoughts on something besides my own misfortunes; but I can find more pleasure in recalling the happy past, and in picturing a brilliant future. For a moment I'm contented; but soon I'm more miserable than ever, and awake to find it but a dream. I cannot look forward to the arrival of the mail, with the most distant hope. I've so often been disappointed, I've quit looking for any.

Our Captain, who has so long been a prisoner at "Johnson's Island", arrived in camp this evening, and as he has kindly offered to take this to Ga., I'm finishing it by a torch light. I'm afraid you can't read it, but I will send it, for if you are as anxious to hear from me, as I am to hear from you (and I doubt not you are), 'twill be a pleasure to look at it whether you can read it or not. Oh Maggie, you can't imagine how very anxious I am to hear from you. It seems as if I hadn't seen or heard from you in years, whereas it has only been *months*. And Oh such months they have been, but I hope 'twill be better soon. Rest assured our silence and separation has not one iota lessened my sincere love for you. I only wish I could prove myself more worthy ---- in me.

I heard this evening that four or five thousand furloughed soldiers of this army were on their way back to rejoin their commands; if this be true, I will surely hear from you. Oh how anxiously I hope I may not be disappointed. Write as often as possible. Love to all your Father's family & my friends and rest assured I'm as ever yours most devoted-

Alva

Penfield, Georgia
10th July 1865
Dearest Maggie,

When I last parted with you, I hoped ere this to have been a regular correspondent; but since the postal system is still incomplete, I will have to resort, for relief, to the Express company. Nothing novel or exciting transpired on my way home. ---- we went to

Houston (one day), I enjoyed myself very much. I saw a *great many* of my old friends. I was offered several schools; but owing to the lateness of the season, I declined; I hadn't forgotten the chills & fever of 1860.

I stopped a day in Covington and my cousin came home with me. Fannie went home with her and during her absence we were quite lonely indeed.

The prospect for an unprecedented large crop of corn is very flattering indeed. At this time, tho', we are suffering a little for rain; but from appearances I think we will have an abundance very soon. The wheat crop is almost an utter failure, a great many farmers not having made as much as was planted. Quite a change has taken place among the negroes since I returned. A great many have left their (homes) to try their fortunes as "Freedmen", and I'm happy to say they've found the way to freedom "a hard road to travel". Many, like the prodigal son, are returning to their homes thoroughly disgusted with everything pertaining to freedom. The had flocked to Greensboro in such numbers that they had become a great nuisance, so much so that the marshal of their town had to make some arrangements to drive them out. A day or two since he went over the town, and arrested & confined in jail *all* old and young male and females who could not show they were engaged in some legitimate employment. It may look incredible; but 80 of this vagrant class were found in one lot, besides others in different places. So many were arrested that the jail was filled to overflowing. After this had been done, the Yankey Provost Marshal ordered that if they would promise to leave the town, they should be released on the following morning. They were, in accordance with the order, let loose and since that time the town seems almost deserted. Any quantity of negores can be hired for their support, they all say they are very sorry they left their homes.

Since I've returned, two gross uncalled for murders have been perpetrated in this county. Recently a negro threatened the life of his master, whereupon several of his neighbors assisted him in arresting

& confining hand & foot this desparate negro, intending to carry him to the Military authorities in Greensboro; but it being nearly night they concluded to wait until morning. During the night a negro in the neighborhood went to the Yankeys and reported that these men had a negro tied and intended to hang him; a guard was immediately dispatched to prevent and to arrest all parties concerned. The guard and having surrounded the house, knocked at the door for admittance. Someone in the house asked "Who's that" the guard replied "I have United States soldiers", the ---- in the house fearing they were negroes refused admittance until they could go out and see and as one of their number walked out of the back door he was shot dead. The whole party was then arrested & sent to Augusta to await their trials. The guard reports they were fired into, when they returned the fire and killed one of the men in the house. The citizens tho' say not a gun was fired except the one fired by the Yankeys. I've no doubt the latter report is correct.

The' second case is more aggravated than the one I've just related. An old and respectable citizen of this county was in his bed asleep, and some one came to his window at about eleven oclock and shot him dead. No one knows of his having had any enemies. 'Tis only known that he kept a crowd of negro dogs and 'tis thought by some that on that account he was killed by negroes, and his own negroes, too, because no one else could have come to the house without its being known. His son, as soon as he found his Father was dead, tried to track the unknown with his dogs, but no trail could be found. This it remains an awful secret, and I suppose ever will. We all ought to be watchful, we know not who are our enemies. And in this connection, Maggie, let me in love request and caution you not to any more expose yourself by going alone so far from home, as you did when you went for the lady who did some sewing for your Mother. You don't know Maggie how I hated to see you go off alone and un-protected, I was almost tempted to ask you to let me go with you; for I knew that the country was full of Yankeys and negroes and that they had no respect for ladies. Will you not for your own personal safety, and for him who loves you more than all earth besides be more careful in future? I know 'tis not always convenient to have someone to accompany you, but recollect to what danger you are exposing yourself, and I think you can always find someone. I've never read of so many acts of violence that it makes my heart shudder to think that you have unknowingly exposed yourself to such indignation. Knowing this I can not help from cautioning you. We now have peaches and watermelons in profusion, and I'm endeavoring to make up the time I've lost during the past four years. I enjoy it finely, I don't think fruit ever tasted so sweet to me before. I know you'll say "take care you'll get sick", I will heed your caution, and eat *lots* of fruit too. You ought to see me eat tomatoes, I'm afraid tho' you'd be ashamed of me. Our vines are more fruitful this year than I've ever before seen them. Tomorrow we will have an exhibition of the *oratorical* powers of the *young gentlemen* going to school here. 'Twill be something like old times! 'Twill be a small "commencement" on a small scale. Balls continue to be the rage in this our once quiet little village. There will be a *"Farewell"* to the students on Tuesday night the 11th.

The happy day for our marriage is fast approaching and yet it *seems* to come oh so slowly, and oh how my heart bounds with joy to know you will soon be my own darling wife. "Joyfully I hail each coming morrow" because I know 'tis one day nearer the consummation of my earthly happiness. Unfavorable as are the surrounding circumstances, we cannot expect happiness, true happiness, but from our mutual love for each other. That each will be to the other, all that heart could wish, I know, and therefore I know we will be happy, very happy.

We have a gloomy future before us, Maggie, but let us not brood over coming difficulties; but rather let our *very troubles* unite us more closely to each other and the sources of happiness instead of pain. Our talking, thinking, or ranting about them will not in the least them; but on the contrary, 'twill embitter us toward everything, everybody, and toward each other. Let us rather each say to the other

"Whate'er fate betide thee my heart still clings to thee". If Fortune should not smile upon us 'tis the will of God, let us not murmur, but with Christianly humility patiently submit, resolving that we *will* court her smiles by more Christianlike conduct.

If nothing serious prevents, I will start for home the 18th or 19th. I cannot tell whether any one will come with me or not. I don't know how *time* will be. Mother, Father, & Sister send their best love. My love to *all* my friends. I'll send this by express to Dr. Everett, he will forward it. If *possible*, write soon dearest one to your devoted.

Alva

P.S. To be in the fashion, I've taken the oath!

A.

Millwood, Georgia
July 23rd 1865
Dearest Alva,

A few days since I was much rejoiced at the reception of your most interesting letter of the 10th inst. Mail facilities not yet having been established, I was beginning to be fearful twould be a long time before I could hear from you. I didn't know we were allowed to send letters by the Express company. You see that is our great disadvantage in living in the "back woods", and so far from the Railroad. We can't keep up with the *times*.

I am glad you had a pleasant time going home and arrived there safely, Oh I know you will help us rejoice. John and Joe are safe at home and quite well. They came on Boat to Savannah and walked from there home. Joe and Jack are having fine times now serenading. You ought to see them flying around. Last week my uncle Mr. Mobley gave them a dancing party. A large crowd were present, and I am sorry to say *lots* of our young church members attended. I didn't attend. I think we do wrong whenever we visit them. What does it show to the world? that we encourage and countenance such. The

Bible says, "we should shun the appearance of evil". I have never attended but one, and that is my last.

One of our Baptist danced the other night at this party, and who do you suppose it was. Lizzie Tomberly. I was never more surprised. Samantha, Babe and Jack danced all night. I took Ma's best to give her consent for them to go. I hope there will be no more in this neighborhood. I can see the evil influence.

Now while I am writing Miss Mollie and Brother are out in the porch with the family, came to sit awhile tonight. I have not been out yet to see them, but must before they leave, provided I finish this letter first.

Pa was glad to receive your letter and that copy. He hasn't made any written agreement with his negroes yet, but will in a few days. One of our negro women, Hannah, has left us, since you were here. The Yankeys sent her home, but Pa made her go back to Hawkinsville, and I hear, has hired to some one in town. The negroes are behaving themselves very well through this section, very few have left their master, in comparison to other sections of this country, and most all that did leave have come back. Pa has taken the oath, and Jack will soon. We have had no Yankeys to see us since you were here, tho they have been in the neighborhood, to see some negroes that wouldn't be controled by their masters.

I thank you for your kind advice, and will heed you. There will be no necessity for my going alone any where now. I have Brothers and cousins too, who will accompany me at any time. There! Mollie has gone and I've not been out yet, well, I will apologize when I next see her.

I went to see Miss Poss Tullington today, and she told me she heard I was to have been married last Sunday morning. Every one I see has either to tell me that they heard I was married or that I was to be soon. They keep guessing, and appointing a time, thinking I reckon that they surely will guess the appointed time after a while. I believe I will surprise them a little after all their much talk,' for about the time appointed, they will not be thinking of it, I am sure. The report will be so old and almost forgotten by the sure enough set time. Unless you write us differently. Pa will send conveyance to Montezuma for you on Monday the 23rd. I've had a glimmering light to write by. Please excuse brevity. I've had but a short time in which to write this letter. I send it off early in the morning to Macon. I hope I shall hear from you again before long. Samantha says she had forgotten all about her promise, but I think she didn't want to remember it. The family *all* send their love. Remember my love to all your Father's family.

I am, dear Alva your own devoted,

Mag

Millwood, Georgia
Sept. 4th 1865
Dearest Alva,

More than two weeks has elapsed since the reception of your last most welcome letter, and I desired much to have responded at an earlier date, but have had no opportunity of sending a letter off. We have been deprived of a regular mail so long at Millwood, I think when the postal system gets completed, we certainly will know how to appreciate it. Yesterday for the first time in a month, we rec'd. our papers. So you may believe we can't keep posted in regard to the *times*; but I think arrangments have been made now for our papers to be brought from Vienna every week, and I do hope twill be done.

Nothing I believe of much interest have transpired since I last wrote. We have all been quite well. For the present protracted meetings are supplanting parties. Quite a revival is going on at Pinehills church and one at Henderson of considerable interest has just closed. But our church members at Harmony[2] are very cold. I think twill take Mr. Horn several days to arouse them to a sense of duty. Last night we had a very interesting preach here, from Mr. Collins, he is improving rapidly. We sent word around to the neighbors and a goodly number were present.

---

[2] Harmony Baptist Church, Millwood (Dooly, Co.) GA

Mr. Harvard is making preparations for a big examination and exhibition at the close of the term, which will be in 6 or 7 weeks. He is using every effort to gain the favor and patronage of the patrons for another School next year. Brother, Samantha and Babe have parts to act in the dialogues. The most interesting and lengthy dialogue is "The Vow fulfilled" perhaps you have seen it. I think twill be very amusing if acted well. There are some 10 or 12 characters. Samantha's part is the most prominent character, and she tried to get Mr. H. to give it to some one else, but he would not. He insisted very much on my taking a part; but I begged off. Most all of the actors are married men and young ladies and young men that are out of the school and some of the patrons are not pleased with the arrangment. Mrs. Henry told me yesterday that Mr. Harvard was injuring his school, instead (of) building it up as he was trying.

Mr. Andrews says he is not going to teach his present school next year. So I know you can get the school if you want it. Pa has spoken to the patrons, for you, for the school, and I guess you will have the refusal. Not knowing how times may be Mr. Harvard may change his intentions at the expiration of this year, and if he should I know you can get *that* school. I know some of the patrons prefer you in preference to him. The school numbers at present from 45 to 50. I don't know of any better country, school.

The tract of land you spoke of was formerly in this county, but now belongs to Wilcox. Pa says all the lands in that district (12th) are very poor.

When I recd. your letter, Pa said if he could get any money he would write to you, to buy him a mule or two also John Graham and Billy Hooks wanted to send with him for you to purchase them some, but as they have not written yet, I presume they can't get any money and I guess they think it uncertain whether there will be any more sales of Government stock soon.

The soldiers (Confederates) seem to think they can't do away with army amusement. A week or two since there was a Tournament at Haynesville. Quite a large crowd was present, and a nice dinner was given.

The gentleman who was the most successful was Mr. Walker from Pulaski. The lady he crowned was an Alabamian. 'Tis said the ladies of Haynesville considered themselves very much slighted by not having the honor confered on them. Several had speeches prepared and you must know they were considerably disappointed. There was to have been another in Perry last week, though I(know) not whether it came off or not.

We are having a nice and sweet time now making sorghum syrup. Pa hasn't any planted; but we make for our neighbors. Mr. Deaton had his made last week. Alex won't come over often now, we accuse Samantha of treating him cold, and really if you know all you would think so. 'Tis really laughable, but I will wait and let her tell you.

Alonzo Baskin was to see Brother last week. He made a trade with Pa and he and Henry Gates will be down again this week. A crowd from this neighborhood left this morning for a fish and deer hunt, 25 miles below this, John and Brother are with the party, we anticipate dining high when they return.

Our candidates for the convention are out flying around. Pa was solicited to run by all his friends most, but he didn't care to do and declined.

I don't know whether I can have the opportunity to write again before the 26th or not but if possible I will. I hope you will soon receive this. Your last was only 5 or 6 days on the way. I am going to send this to Vienna tomorrow to a gentleman who will express it for me.

If possible you must bring your Sister, and Cousin with you. Give my love to all the family. All here send much love to you.

Write soon to your most devoted-

Maggie

CHAPTER SEVEN

1866

These three letters from Alva's parents explain the events of the day, and the thoughts of this Georgia family entering the post-war era. Alva and Margaret set up home in Dooly County, and begin their family. The hardships of farming, making ends meet, and many of the challenges they faced are much the same as they are today for rural farming families everywhere.

Penfield
Mar. 19th 1866
Dear Alva & Maggie,

Your Ma has just finished a letter and says as she has written scarcely anything, I *must write* a few lines at least. Last night was snapping cold, and if the fruit is not killed in the bud, it will be on account of the dryness of the atmosphere. Our strawberry bed, now beginning to bloom, was covered with frost this morning. But I can perceive no injury yet. This evening the weather seems to have moderated, the wind having changed from N.W. (a cold quarter) to the Southwest.

You made some enquiry in your last letter about the freedmen, how they were doing, etc. Well, they are an indolent, restless, dissatisfied race; and in this present condition, with the privilege of refusing to work if they choose to do so, they are not to be relied on or trusted out of sight.

We have not heard anything from Abram since he left & therefore know nothing of his whereabouts, nor are we anxious to hear. I hear almost every day of some violating their contracts, leaving their employers & seeking for higher wages. This they will continue to do, notwithstanding the *friendly oversight* & faithful watchcare of the Freedmen's Bureau. Your Ma has written you of the sudden death of Mrs. Cramer, a sad affliction indeed to the numerous family she has left behind. Joe and Tom have rented some land of May McWhorter this year & are farming on what is called the Brockman's place near Mr. Chiren's. They have employed some negroes for a share of the crop and are said to be doing very well. They built some houses on the place and one or both of their oldest sisters stay out there with them. Ma & Fannie are already anticipating a visit from you & Maggie next summer. Love to Maggie & all the family.

Affectionately yrs. truly,
B. E. Spencer
(Letter from Alva's father, Benjamin Edgar Spencer)

Penfield Sept 17th 1866

Dear Alva & Maggie

Your last letters came to hand a day or two since, and as usual, there was a strife between your Ma & Fannie, each one desiring to read them first. We were glad to learn that you were both well & in cheerful spirits, and that your school continues to flourish.

We have a good deal of wet weather, so that our short cotton crops are already considerably injured by the frequent rains. The opening bowls are near the ground and the rain not only stains the lint, but scatters it so that a good deal of it is lost. There will be but little cotton made in this county, not more than 1/4 of the usual crop.

Corn is very short, mostly *nubbings*. A good many up-land fields when the ground was not well worked are almost completely cut off. I suppose, on an average, there will not be a half crop. But since the rains have set in the people have sown large turnip patches and a great many will sow Barley & Rye lots, and sow all the hay they can to make up the deficiency of corn & shucks. The great difficulty will be in fattening hogs; for there is no *mast* this year and the pea crop is almost entirely cut off. But the people will have to kill their hogs whether they yield lard or not. I think I will have corn enough to fatten mine as I have kept them in good order all summer.

Our Superior Court was held in this county last week and continued till Saturday evening before it adjourned. One criminal case occupied the court nearly three days. A brother of Dr. Frank Durham, (I think they called him General) was shot about ten days ago at Sciell Shoals by a man named Harper. He lived about two days. Harper was arrested & tried for murder but was cleared. A few days previous to the Shooting it seems that they had a difficulty, after which Durham threatened to kill Harper even if he had to go & commit the deed in his own house. Accordingly he went to Harper's house with a double barrel shot gun & a pistol bound around him to carry his threat into execution, as he said to several persons while on his way. Harper had heard of his threats & was prepared for him. When he arrived at the house and got into the yard. Harper took his shot gun, went out into the yard & shot him. These are about the facts as testified to by the witnesses. Durham had been drinking for several days previous, and also at the time he went to Harper's house. So it seems that liquor was foundation of the difficulty and the remote cause of his untimely death. Durham, when sober, was an inoffensive fellow. But when intoxicated, like everybody else, he was a fool.

Tucker has not yet returned from the North, and is not expected till sometime in November. From present appearances, the college will not flourish much under his administration during this term. Brantly has not yet accepted his appointment to the Professorship of

Belle Letters, tho' it is thought that perhaps he will & be ready for the spring term.

Love to Maggie, Babe and all the family.

Affectionately yours truly

B.E. Spencer

Penfield 16th Dec. 1866

My Dear Son & Daughter,

It is Sunday evening, and very unpleasant. Since yesterday morning we have nothing but sleet, rain, & wind, and it has been as much as we could do to keep comfortable. There has been no preaching and if there had been, your Pa would not have been able to go, he strained his hip or side when he killed hogs, and is quite lame, & suffers considerable with it. I am sorry to tell you that Mr. Robinson is almost entirely confined to his bed, seems to be declining fast. He is so weak & feeble that he cannot take medicine, which he thinks he needs. I hope he will rally yet, tho I do not think there is much prospect of it. If he should die, I know of no one that would be as much missed. Mrs. Lindsey is very feeble and I hardly think she can live thro' the winter. Dennis S. has been once to see us. Expects to return to Mitchel before Christmas. They had a little party there last Thursday night. Fannie went with Marian, Cliff & Jerry. I think I wrote you that Doct. Harris is to teach the female school. Has moved into the Academy house. Mitchel moved into the Armstrong house. Mr. Colelough has rented the store room in Beasley house, opens a store tomorrow. Mostly groceries now, but expects to have a large next year I think. I suppose he will sell right smart in the Christmas, as you know every body that can raise 10 cts. will spend it then. You do not know how anxious we are to hear from you, do try to find some way to send a letter oftener. You know we cannot help being anxious now. We suppose you have got moved "home", we have been wondering what you are doing this cold rainy day. Mrs. Lunford & Charley are with Anna I suppose as they left for there on Thursday I think. Proff expects to be there at Christmas. The trip would not be much if money were not so scarce. Gus Sharpe I think I wrote you had gone to Florida, he was improving when they heard last. Mrs. Tucker will probably be here this week. I hope dear Maggie, you will not be so ambitious in your new home as to exert yourself too much, let things take their course until you get well, then you can fly round as much as you please. I am afraid you will be rather lonely at first, after having so many at home but I hope & trust you will enjoy each other's society the better. I hoped to be able to give you family Bible before you commenced housekeeping, but it is out my power at present. I hope & trust you have consecrated your house as well as yourselves over to God, May you dwell under His shadow always. Dr. Morgan has bought a house in Greensboro and will probably move there in the spring, a foolish move I think, but he knows his own business best. I think Aunt May will stay another year with us, tho I do not know certain. She sends love. All your friends send love. Give our love to Babe and all the family. Sis will write.

Affy. Mother C.G.Spencer

(Letter from Alva's mother, Charlotte Griffin (Hurd) Spencer)

In Memoriam

Obituary

Died at his residence in Dooly county, Ga., on the 20th day of May, 1881, Alva B. Spencer, aged forty years.

Mr. Spencer came from the county of Greene to this county at the age of 21 years, engaging in teaching school at harmony church in 1861, but the late war breaking out, he enlisted and served during the war, at the close of which he returned home, and married the eldest daughter of Judge W. B. Cone, where he resided until his death.

He embraced the Baptist faith at Penfield church in 1858, then but exemplifying the one predominant principle of his youth, which was distinguished by the most conscientious and tender regard for his parents and the precepts of the Bible, presage of his future felicity. His entire youth was tempered with the most winning modesty and engaging respect. His children, he early sought to instill in them the faith and fear of the Almighty Father. As when pale and emaciated he sat upon his death-bed he requested that his family assemble, when, with the precious remaining breaths, he admonished his children to filial duty and that faith through which they might hope to meet him in a better and happier land. It pleased God to give him a long foresight of his approaching dissolution by means of that slow, lingering disease, consumption.[1] Yet with what Christian fortitude did he bear his sad affliction. Never did he, until his early dissolution became apparent to all, make any mention of his serious illness, and then alone in terms that showed his satisfaction of a better home above.

---

[1] Tuberculosis.

His only regret in dying, as he often stated, was that of leaving his family. His sickness was borne with such faith and all the cheerful resignation and patience which is pecular to a true Christian.

His punctuality, honesty and worth caused him to serve in many places of honor and trust among his fellow men.

In his death his companion has lost a loving husband, his children a devoted parent, the poor a sympathising and open-handed friend, and the church an amiable and true Christian. He has gone. The tender heart must bleed and the affectionate eye cannot fail to drop a tear. Yet look forward and behold, see in the joyful realms his spirit resting among friends immortal and unchangeable greeting his arrival. And 'twill be but a greater joy to him to stand at the gate and welcome the happy spirits of those he left on earth weeping.   R.R.   Eureka, Ga., August 8, 1881

Hawkinsville Dispatch (Hawkinsville, Ga.,) August 25, 1881

SOURCES

Alva Benjamin Spencer diary, 6 Sept 1861 – 1 Oct 1861. Floyd
Mashburn Turk private collection. Waycross, Georgia.

Alva Benjamin Spencer letters, 1861 – 1865. Floyd Mashburn Turk
private collection. Waycross, Georgia.

Andrew Jackson Cone letters, 14 May 1863 and 20 Oct 1864. Floyd
Mashburn Turk private collection. Waycross, Georgia.

Benjamin Edgar Spencer letters, 1866. Floyd Mashburn Turk private
collection. Waycross, Georgia.

Charlotte Griffin (Hurd) Spencer letters, 1866. Floyd Mashburn
Turk private collection. Waycross, Georgia.

Margaret Lucinda Cone letters, 1861 – 1865. Floyd Mashburn Turk
private collection. Waycross, Georgia.

No Author. "American Affairs," News reported in the style of a letter
from the field. *The Times* London, 17 July 1862, 7.

No Author. "Before Petersburg." *Harper's Weekly* New York, 20 Aug
1864,1. Available on
http://www.sonofthesouth.net/leefoundation/the-civil-war.htm.

No Author. Obituary of Alva Benjamin Spencer. *Hawkinsville
Dispatch* Hawkinsville, Georgia, 25 August 1881. Available on
microfilm at the University of Georgia Hargrove Library.
Athens, Georgia.

Thomas J. Cone letters, 1862. Floyd Mashburn Turk private
collection. Waycross, Georgia.

INDEX